TABLE OF CONTENTS

Day mercantilism 2
Professional day tradering 7
Trading coding 11
ECNs and exchanges 16
Personality and Temperament: 22
guerrilla mercantilism 30
finding the right stocks for day mercantilism 41
Risk Management 52
Contrarian finance 60
Different Parties and Spreads 67
order entry, exit and trade management 75
Bull Flag 84
Algorithmic traders 112

DAY MERCANTILISM

Day mercantilism is theory in securities, specifically buying and commerce financial instruments within constant commerce day, such all positions square measure closed before the market closes for the commerce day. Traders WHO modification this capability with the motive of profit square measure therefore speculators. The ways in which of quick mercantilism distinction with the semi-permanent trades underlying get and hold and price finance ways. Day traders exit positions before the market shuts to avoid unmanageable risks and negative worth gaps between one day's shut and so following day's value at the open.

Day traders generally North American natione margin leverage; inside the us, Regulation T permits associate initial most leverage of 2:1, but many brokers will permit 4:1 leverage as long as a result of the leverage is reduced to 2:1 or less by the highest of the mercantilism day. inside the North American nation, of us that make quite four day trades per week square measure termed pattern day traders and square measure required to require care of $25,000 in equity in their accounts.[1] Since margin interest is sometimes exclusively charged on long balances, the businessperson might pay no interest fees for the margin profit, though' still running the danger of a requirement. Margin interest rates square measure generally supported the broker's call.

Some of loads of normally day-traded financial instruments square measure stocks, options, currencies, contracts for distinction, and a bunch of futures contracts like equity index futures, charge per unit futures, currency futures and product futures.

Day mercantilism was once associate activity that was exclusive to financial firms and trained speculators. many day traders square measure bank or fund staff operative as specialists in equity investment and fund management. Day mercantilism gained quality once the liberation of commissions inside the U.S in 1975, the looks of electronic mercantilism platforms inside the 19 Nineties, and with the stock worth volatility throughout the dot-com bubble. sometime merchandisers use associate intra-day technique observed as scalping that generally has the merchant holding a footing for a handful of minutes or exclusively seconds.

There was once a time once the only of us that were able to trade actively inside the stock market were those operative for large cash institutions, brokerages, and mercantilism homes. But, with the rise of cyberspace and on-line mercantilism homes, brokers have created it easier for the common individual capitalist to urge in on the game.

Day mercantilism can sway be a awfully profitable career, as long as you're doing it properly. but it can also be a small amount tough for novices— particularly for those who are not completely prepared with a well-planned strategy. Even the foremost seasoned day traders can hit rough patches and ability losses. So, what specifically is day mercantilism and therefore the means can it work?

- Day traders square measure active traders WHO execute intraday ways to profit off value changes for a given and.
- Day mercantilism employs an honest sort of techniques and

- ways to use perceived market inefficiencies.
- Day mercantilism is sometimes characterised by technical analysis and wishes a high degree of self-discipline and perspicacity.

Day mercantilism is made public as a result of the acquisition and sale of a security at intervals one mercantilism day. it'll occur in any marketplace but is most common inside the interchange (forex) and stock markets. Day traders square measure typically educated and well-funded. They use high amounts of leverage and short mercantilism ways to use very little value movements in very liquid stocks or currencies. Day traders square measure attuned to events that cause short market moves. mercantilism the news can be a popular technique. Regular announcements like economic statistics, company earnings or interest rates square measure subject to market expectations and market science. Markets react once those expectations are not met or square measure exceeded, generally with unexpected, important moves, which can profit day traders.

Day traders use numerous intraday ways. These ways include:

- Scalping, that tries to make numerous very little profits on little prices changes throughout the day
- Range mercantilism, that primarily uses support and resistance levels to ascertain their get and sell choices
- News-based mercantilism, that usually seizes mercantilism opportunities from the heightened volatility around news events

- High-frequency mercantilism (HFT) ways that use refined algorithms to require advantage of very little or short market inefficiencies

The profit potential of day mercantilism is perhaps one amongst the foremost debated and misunderstood topics on Wall Street. internet day mercantilism scams have lured amateurs by promising large returns throughout a brief quantity. the construct that this type of mercantilism can be a get-rich-quick theme persists. Some of us day trade whereas not enough info. but there square measure day traders WHO build a lucky living despite—or perhaps as a results of of—the risks.

Many trained money managers and cash advisors recoil from day mercantilism competition that, in most cases, the reward does not justify the danger. Conversely, those who do day trade insist there is profit to be created. Day mercantilism profitably is feasible; but the success rate is inherently lower as a results of the standard and necessary risk of day mercantilism in conjunction with the connected scams. Moreover, economists and cash practitioners alike argue that over whereas periods, active mercantilism ways tend to underperform a loads of basic passive index strategy, significantly once fees and taxes square measure taken into thought.

Day mercantilism is not for everyone and involves important risks. Moreover, it desires an intensive and in-depth understanding of but the markets work and varied ways for profiting inside the short term. whereas we have a tendency to tend to stay in mind the success stories of those WHO smitten it loaded as day after day dealer, detain mind that the bulk do not—many will discontinue and lots of can merely barely keep afloat. Moreover, do not underestimate the role that luck and smart temporal property play—while talent is truly a component; a rout of unhealthy luck can sink even the foremost knowledgeable day dealer.

PROFESSIONAL DAY TRADERING

Professional day traders—those WHO trade for a living rather than as a hobby—are usually well-established inside the sphere. they generally have in-depth info of the marketplace, too. Here square measure variety of the stipulations required to be a lucky day trader:

Individuals WHO conceive to day trade whereas not associate understanding of market fundamentals generally loses money. Technical analysis and chart reading can be a wise ability for every day dealer to possess, but whereas not a loads of in-depth understanding of the market you are in and so the assets that exist during this market, charts is additionally deceiving. Do your due diligence and understand the particular ins and outs of the merchandise you trade

Day traders use exclusively assets that they're going to afford to lose. Not exclusively can this defend them from liquidation, but it collectively helps eliminate feeling from their commerce. associate large amount of capital is often necessary to capitalize effectively on intraday worth movements. Having access to a account is in addition key, since volatile swings can incur margin calls on short notice.

A dealer needs a grip over the rest of the market. There square measure several utterly other ways day traders use also as swing commerce, arbitrage, and mercantilism news. These ways in which square measure refined until they end up consistent profits and effectively limit losses.

A profitable strategy is useless whereas not discipline. many day traders notice themselves losing an excellent deal of money as a results of they fail to create trades that meet their own criteria. As they are saying, "Plan the trade and trade the organize." Success isn't attainable whereas not discipline.

To profit, day traders bank heavily on volatility inside the market. A stock is additionally attractive to every day dealer if it moves an excellent deal throughout the day. that may happen because of style of numerous things also as associate profitand-loss statement, capitalist sentiment, or even general economic or company news.

Day traders collectively like stocks that square measure heavily liquid as a results of that gives them the prospect to change their position whereas not sterilization the price of the stock. If a stock worth moves higher, traders would possibly take a get position. If the price moves down, a dealer would possibly arrange to short-sell so he can profit once it falls.

Regardless of what technique day after day dealer uses, they are generally attempting to trade a stock that moves... a lot.

There square measure a pair of primary divisions of trained day traders: those who work alone and/or those that work for a much bigger institution. Most day traders WHO trade for a living work for associate large institution. These traders have a bonus as a results of they have access to an instantaneous line, a commerce table, large amounts of capital and leverage, expensive analytical coding system, and much loads of. These traders square measure usually checking out easy profits which will be created from arbitrage opportunities and news events, and these resources allow them to require advantage of those less risky day trades before individual traders can react.

Individual traders generally manage different people's money or simply trade with their own. Few of them have access to a commerce table; but they generally have durable ties to a brokerage (due to the massive amounts they pay on commissions) and access to different resources. However, the restricted scope of these resources prevents them from competitive directly with institutional day traders. Instead, they are forced to need loads of risks. Individual traders usually day trade exploitation technical analysis and swing trades—combined with some leverage—to generate adequate profits on such little worth movements in very liquid stocks.

Day commerce demands access to variety of the foremost difficult cash services and instruments inside the marketplace. Day traders usually require:

This is generally reserved for traders operative massive|for big} institutions or those who manage large amounts of money. The dealing table provides these traders with quick order executions that square measure notably necessary once sharp worth movements occur. as an example, once a buying deal is declared, day traders gazing merger arbitrage can place their orders before the rest of the market is in an exceedingly position to need advantage of the price differential.

News provides the majority of opportunities from that day traders capitalize; so it's imperative to be the first to know once one factor vital happens. the quality mercantilism area contains access to the DowJones Industrial Average Newswire, constant coverage of CNBC and different news organizations, and coding system that constantly analyzes news sources for necessary stories.

TRADING CODING

Trading coding system could be a trendy necessity for several day traders. those who settle for technical indicators or swing trades bank loads of on coding system than news. This coding system is additionally characterised by the following:

- Automatic pattern recognition: this suggests the commerce program identifies technical indicators like flags and channels, or loads of difficult indicators like Elliott Wave patterns.

- Genetic and neural applications: These square measure programs that use neural networks and genetic algorithms to glorious commerce systems to create loads of correct predictions of future worth movements.

- Broker integration: variety of those applications even interface directly with the brokerage that allows for associate on the spot and even automatic execution of trades. usually|this can be} often helpful for eliminating feeling from commerce and up execution times.

- Back testing: this allows traders to seem at but a particular strategy would have performed within the past thus on predict loads of accurately however it will perform within the future. Confine in mind that past performance is not invariably indicative of future results.

Combined, these tools offer traders with a grip over the rest of the marketplace.

It's easy to ascertain why, whereas not them, various inexperienced traders lose money.

As mentioned over, day mercantilism as a career is also very hard and quite challenge. First, you would like to return back in with some info of the commerce world and have a good set up of your risk tolerance, capital, and goals.

Day mercantilism is in addition a career that desires an excellent deal of it slow. If you would like to glorious your strategies—after you have practiced, of course—and build money, you'll need to be compelled to devote an excellent deal of it slow to that. this is not one factor you will do part-time or whenever you get the urge. you have got need to be entirely blessed in it.

If you're doing decide that the thrill of commerce is correct for you, bear in mind to begin out little. Target several stocks rather than going into the market head-first and sporting yourself skinny. Going all out will exclusively complicate your commerce strategy and should mean huge losses.

Finally, keep cool and take a glance at to remain the sensation out of your trades. The loads of you will do this, the loads of you will be able to continue your organize. Keeping level head permits you to stay up your focus whereas keeping you on the path you have elite to travel down.

If you follow these easy pointers, you may be headed for a good career in day commerce.

Because of the character of financial leverage and conjointly the quick returns that square measure accomplishable, day mercantilism results can vary from terribly profitable to very unprofitable, and unsound profile traders can generate either massive share returns or large share losses. attributable to the high profits (and losses) that day mercantilism makes accomplishable, these traders square measure usually pictured as "bandits" or "gamblers" by completely different investors.

Day mercantilism is risky, significantly if any of the next is gift whereas trading: mercantilism a loser's game/system rather than a game that is a minimum of winnable, inadequate capital with the connected excess stress of about to "survive", incompetent money management (i.e. execution trades poorly).

The common use of buying on margin (using borrowed funds) amplifies gains and losses, such substantial losses or gains can occur throughout a} terribly short quantity of it slow. in addition, brokers generally alter larger margin for day traders. inside the North American nation as associate example, whereas the initial margin required to hold a stock position long square measure 5 hundredth of the stock's value because of Regulation T, many brokers alter pattern day bargainer accounts to use levels as low as twenty fifth for intraday purchases. this suggests on a commonplace bargainer with the legal minimum $25,000 in his account should purchase $100,000 (4x leverage) worth of stock throughout the day, as long as 1/2 those positions square measure exited before the market shut. because of the high risk of margin use, and of various day mercantilism practices, on a commonplace bargainer will generally need to exit a losing position very quickly, thus on stop a much bigger, unacceptable loss, or maybe a unfortunate loss, loads of larger than her original investment, or maybe larger than her total assets.

Originally, the foremost important U.S. stocks were listed on the NY exchange. A merchant would contact an element, WHO would relay the order to a specialist on the bottom of the massive board. These specialists would each build markets in only one or 2 of stocks. The specialist would match the consumer with another broker's seller; write up physical tickets that, once processed, would effectively transfer the stock; and relay the information back to every broker. Before 1975, brokerage commissions were mounted at I Chronicles of the quantity of the trade, i.e. to buy $10,000 value of stock worth the client $100 in commissions and same I Chronicles to sell. which means that to profit trades had to create over book to create any real gain.

One of the first steps to create day mercantilism of shares likely profitable was the modification inside the commission theme. In 1975, the u. s. Securities and Exchange Commission (SEC) created mounted commission rates outlaw, giving rise to discount brokers giving loads of reduced commission rates.

Financial settlement periods accustomed be loads of longer: Before the primary Nineties at the London exchange, as an example, stock is got up to 10 operative days once it completely was bought, allowing traders to buy for (or sell) shares at the beginning of a settlement amount exclusively to sell (or buy) them before the tip of the quantity hoping for a rise in worth. This activity was the image of modern mercantilism, apart from the longer amount of the settlement amount. But today, to cut back market risk, the settlement quantity is sometimes a pair of operative days. Reducing the settlement quantity reduces the possibility of default, but wasn't attainable before the arrival of electronic possession transfer.

The systems by that stocks square measure listed have collectively evolved, the half the twentieth century having seen the arrival of transmission networks (ECNs). These square measure primarily large proprietary computer networks on it brokers can list a definite amount of securities to sell at a definite value (the terms or "ask") or offer to buy for a definite quantity of securities at a definite value (the "bid").

ECNS AND EXCHANGES

ECNs and exchanges square measure generally known to traders by a three- or four-letter designators, that establish the ECN or exchange on Level II stock screens. the first of these was Instinet (or "inet"), that was supported in 1969 as a way for major institutions to bypass the additional and additional cumbersome and expensive massive board, and to allow them to trade throughout hours once the exchanges were closed.[6] Early ECNs like Instinet were very unfriendly to little investors, as a results of they attended provide large institutions higher prices than were accessible to the overall public. This resulted throughout a fragmented and generally illiquid market.

The next important step in facilitating day mercantilism was the initiation in 1971 of NASDAQ—a virtual exchange on it orders were transmitted electronically. Moving from paper share certificates and written share registers to "dematerialized" shares, traders used processed mercantilism and registration that needed not exclusively intensive changes to legislation but collectively the event of the obligatory technology: on-line and real time systems rather than batch; electronic communications instead of the communication, telex or the physical consignment of computer tapes, and conjointly the event of secure science algorithms.

These developments publicized the appearance of "market makers": the National Association of Securities Dealers machine-driven Quotations equivalent of an enormous board specialist. A market maker incorporates a list of stocks to buy for and sell, and at a similar time offers to buy for and sell an identical stock. Obviously, it will offer to sell stock at a more robust value than the worth at that it offers to buy for. This distinction is believed as a result of the "spread". The market maker is indifferent on whether or not or not the stock goes up or down, it simply tries to constantly purchase for fewer than it sells. A persistent trend in one direction will finish in an exceedingly loss for the market maker; but the strategy is overall positive (otherwise they'd exit the business). of late there square measure relating to 5 hundred firms United Nations agency participate as market makers on ECNs, each generally making a market in four to forty utterly completely different stocks. with none legal obligations, market makers were free to offer smaller spreads on transmission networks than on the National Association of Securities Dealers machine-driven Quotations. atiny low capitalist might have to pay a $0.25 unfold (e.g. he might have to pay $10.50 to buy for a share of stock but would possibly exclusively get $10.25 for selling it), whereas an institution would exclusively pay a $0.05 unfold (buying at $10.40 and selling at $10.35).

Following the 1987 exchange crash, the SEC adopted "Order Handling Rules" that required market makers to publish their best bid and rise on the National Association of Securities Dealers machine-driven Quotations. Another reform created was the "Small-order execution system", or "SOES", that required market makers to buy for or sell, in real time, little orders (up to at least one thousand shares) at the market maker's listed bid or raise. the design of the system gave rise to arbitrage by atiny low cluster of traders known as the "SOES bandits", WHO created sizable profits buying and selling little orders to plug makers by anticipating worth moves before they were reflected inside the written inside bid/ask prices. The SOES system ultimately diode to mercantilism fast by software package instead of market makers via ECNs

In the late Nineties, existing ECNs began to provide their services to little investors. New ECNs arose, most importantly solid ground (NYSE Arca) Instinet, SuperDot, and Island ECN. solid ground eventually became a exchange and in 2005 was purchased by the massive board.

Electronic mercantilism platforms were created and commissions plummeted. a web monger in 2005 might have bought $300,000 value of stock at a commission of however $10, compared to the $3,000 commission the monger would have paid in 1974. Moreover, the monger was in an exceedingly position in 2005 to buy for the stock nearly instantly and got it at a more cost-effective worth.

This combination of things has created day mercantilism in stocks and stock derivatives (such as ETFs) potential. The low commission rates alter a private or little firm to create associate large style of trades throughout in the future. The liquidity and little spreads provided by ECNs alter a private to create near-instantaneous trades and to induce favorable valuation.

The ability for folks to day trade coincided with the extraordinary industry in technological issues from 1997 to early 2000, known as the dotcom bubble. From 1997 to 2000, the National Association of Securities Dealers machine-driven Quotations rose from 1200 to 5000. many naive investors with little market experience created massive profits buying these stocks within the morning and selling them within the afternoon, at 400th margin rates.

In March 2000, this bubble burst, associated an large style of lessexperienced day traders began to lose money as fast, or faster, than that they'd created throughout the buying mania. The National Association of Securities Dealers machine-driven Quotations crashed from 5000 back to 1200; many of the less-experienced traders went bust, tho' clearly it completely was potential to possess created a fortune throughout that time by short selling or collaborating in on volatility.

In parallel to stock mercantilism, starting at the tip of the Nineties, several new market maker firms provided exchange and by-product day mercantilism through electronic mercantilism platforms. These allowed day traders to possess instant access to decentralised markets like forex and world markets through derivatives like contracts for distinction. Most of these firms were based inside the good United Kingdom of Great Britain and Northern Ireland and later in less restrictive jurisdictions, this was partly attributable to the laws inside the North yank country prohibiting this type of over-the-counter mercantilism. These firms typically offer mercantilism on margin allowing day traders to need large position with relatively great letter, but with the associated increase in risk. The retail exchange mercantilism became a la mode to day trade attributable to its liquidity and conjointly the 24hour nature of the market.

Short holding time/No long holding: the term "holding" refers to the stock you are mercantilism. inside the case of day mercantilism, you will exclusively hold the stock in its "position" (in mercantilism, the position refers to associate agreement by the holder to either purchase or sell that certain quantity of stock) for the amount of it slow that the market is open (9:30am to 4pm). This amounts to simply to a lower place a vi.5 hours of holding time. As we have coated, holding the position for this specific time frame protects your stock from any long fluctuations (risk) inside the market---a time when you can not trade anyway). Once you close up up out your last trade for the day, you are primarily done until you trade another time resulting morning.

Expensive startup costs: Day mercantilism desires some up-front parts which is able to quickly add up in worth. Mercantilism accounts want a minimum of $25,000 for a dealer to create any trade, this amount should be viable thus on keep your mercantilism access open. you may conjointly need mercantilism capital to essentially build the trades--- and amount which will vary greatly for beginners, but it's recommended you begin with a minimum of $500 to $2500.

The higher than quoted refers to exclusively the essential worth to initiate associate account and start mercantilism. inside following chapter we'll cowl the importance of putting in place a digital that incorporates a high performance laptop and a quick web affiliation. If you're doing not already possess these components, you may need to be compelled to take a position in them quickly. Finally, there is education and training. It's prompt {that you|that you merely|that you just} simply take each day mercantilism course from a honored trainer, or, once you become well skilled, you'll have to require a grip in classes to hone your skills. Quality coaching would possibly worth anywhere from $2,000 or loads of depending on the content. costlier commissions and fees: this might be since you'll be doing loads of trades, and you'll be mercantilism day after day. Paying fees for each trade would possibly take associate large chunk from your earnings—these vary from 20-30% depending on the quantity of service that is provided. it'll be to your advantage to comparison search, or to hunt out firms which will offer special discounts if you opened your trade account with them.

Earnings square measure combined loads of quickly: here could be a few good news, day mercantilism offers a faster come back on your earnings that in turn, generate any earnings. If you are making winning trade, you may see daily feedback in your account, and this may feel immensely gratifying.

PERSONALITY AND TEMPERAMENT:

Personality and Temperament: square measure you able to sit and concentrate on an excellent kind of amount, streaming data for hours at a time? square measure you willing to forgo a regular work-life with company edges and support? we have already coated the essential personal qualities of self-discipline and independence required for a winning day dealer. chances are high that, if you are reading this book, you attainable have a temperament that values autonomy and enjoys the instant feedback (negative or positive) that holy day mercantilism offers. You really get pleasure from the thought of operative arduous as a results of there is a chance that the payoff is staggeringly profitable.

Lifestyle and Quality of Life: depending on the type of modus vivendi you'd enjoy; day mercantilism are either your worst nightmare or a dream come back true. If you are the kind of one WHO counts on regular vacation days and predictable gain streams, then attainable you may understand day mercantilism a difficult fit---but if you relish the prospect of seeing your portfolio likely grow to new heights and square measure willing to permit lean times, then day mercantilism is your best be.

In this chapter {i will|i will be able to|i'll} be able to review many of the basics of day mercantilism and hopefully answer your queries on what day mercantilism is and therefore the means it works. The chapter also will introduce variety of the foremost tools and techniques that you'll come upon later inside the book. like all kind, tools square measure of no value unless you acknowledge the way to use them. This book is your guide in learning some way to use these tools.

A compelling question to begin with is: What do you hunt for as each day trader? the solution is easy. First, you're checking out stocks that are becoming a comparatively sure manner. Secondly, you are about to trade them in in some some time within the future. you may not keep any position long. If you get stock in Apple opposition. (ticker: AAPL) today, as associate example, you will not hold your position long and sell it tomorrow. If you hold onto any stock long, it's not day mercantilism, it's known as swing mercantilism.

Swing mercantilism is also a kind of mercantilism inside that you hold stocks over a quantity of your time, typically from in some some time within the future to a handful of weeks. It's a really entirely completely different sort of mercantilism, and you shouldn't use the ways in which and tools simply} just use for day mercantilism to do and do swing commerce. do you detain mind Rule two; where i mentioned that day mercantilism is also a business? Swing mercantilism is in addition a business, but a really completely different moderately business. The variations between swing mercantilism and day mercantilism square measure a similar because the variations in owning a construction and a food delivery company. They every involve food, but they are very completely different: they operate with different time frames, laws, market segments and revenue models. you ought to not confuse day mercantilism with completely different sorts of mercantilism just because the mercantilism involves stocks. Day traders incessantly shut their positions before the market closes.

Many traders, also as I, do day after day mercantilism and swing mercantilism. we have a tendency to square measure aware that we've got an inclination to square measure running a pair of entirely completely different businesses, which we've got seasoned separate tutorial programs for the two sorts of mercantilism. one in each of the key variations between day mercantilism and swing mercantilism is that the approach to stock selecting. i do not swing trade and day trade constant stocks. Swing traders typically hunt for stocks in solid companies that they acknowledge won't lose their entire worth long.

For day mercantilism, however, you will trade one thing, as well as firms which will shortly go bankrupt; as a results of you don't care what happens when the market closes. In fact, many of the companies simply} just day trade square measure too risky to hold long as a results of they may lose bumper of their value during this in need of a quantity of it slow. you have got presently reached Rule 3 of day trading:

Rule 3: Day traders do not hold positions long. If necessary, you wish to sell with a loss to make sure you're doing not hold onto any stock long.

Day traders acquire stocks inside the hope that their worth will go higher. this could be referred to as shopping for long, or simply long. when you hear American state or a fellow businessperson voice communication, "I am long 100 shares AAPL," it means that we've bought 100 shares of Apple opposition. And would adore to sell them higher for a profit. Going long is good once the market goes higher. however what if prices square measure dropping? during this case, you will sell short and still build a profit. Day traders can borrow shares from their broker and sell them, hoping that the price can go lower that they'll then acquire those shares back at a cheaper price and build a profit. this could be referred to as mercantilism, or simply short. once folks say, "I am short Apple," it suggests that they have sold-out short stocks of Apple and that they hope that prices will drop. Once the price goes lower, you owe 100 shares to your broker (it possibly shows as -100 shares in your account), which implies you wish to return back 100 shares of Apple to your broker. Your broker doesn't need your money; they need their shares back. So, if the price has gone lower, you'll be able to acquire them cheaper than you bought them earlier and build a profit

Imagine simply} just borrow 100 shares of Apple from your broker and sell them at $100 per share. Apple's worth then drops to $90, therefore you go back to those 100 shares at $90 and are available back them to your broker. you have got got created $10/share or $1,000. What if the price of Apple goes up to $110? during this case, you still need to get 100 shares to return back to your broker as a results of you owe them shares and not cash. Therefore, you have got need to buy 100 shares at $110 thus on return one hundred shares to your broker. during this case, you'll need lost $1,000.

Short sellers profit once the price of the stock they borrowed and sold-out drops. short sale is extremely vital as a results of stock prices generally drop far more quickly than they go up. Concern is also an extra powerful feeling than greed. Therefore, short sellers, if they trade right, can build astonishing profits whereas completely different traders panic and begin to dump.

However, like one thing inside the market that has nice potential, mercantilism has its risks too. Once buying stocks of a company for $5, the worst case state of affairs is that the company goes bankrupt and you lose your $5. there is a limit to your loss. but if you short sell that company at $5 so the price, instead of taking place, starts going higher and higher, then there won't be any limit to your loss. the worth might attend $10, $20, or $100, and still there will be no limit to your loss. Your broker desires those shares back. Not exclusively square measure you able to lose all of the money in your account; but your broker may additionally sue you for more money if you are doing not have adequate funds to cover your shorts.

Short selling is also a legal activity for several smart reasons. First, it provides the markets with extra information. Short sellers typically complete intensive and bonafide due diligence to seek out facts and flaws that support their suspicion that the corporate is overvalued. If there are no short sellers, the price of stocks would possibly immoderately increase higher and higher. Short sellers square measure equalization the market and adjusting prices to their low-cost value. Their actions square measure causative to the health of the market. If the price goes to travel lower, you may properly raise, why can your broker permit you to short sell instead of selling stock themselves before the price drops?

The answer is that the broker would adore to hold their position for the long run. short sale provides investors WHO own the stock (with long positions) with the power to return up with more gain by disposal their shares to the shorts. long run investors WHO build their shares out there for temporary commerce do not appear to be terrified of short term ups and downs. they have blessed inside the corporate for associate honest reason and that they don't have any interest in commerce their shares throughout a brief quantity of it slow. They so like better to lend their shares to traders WHO would love to make a benefit of short term fluctuations of the market. In exchange for disposal their shares, they'll charge interest. Therefore, by trading, you will need to pay some interest to your broker as a result of the worth of borrowing those shares.

If you short sell solely throughout constant day, you usually will not need to pay any interest. Swing traders WHO sell short, generally have to be compelled to pay daily interest on their short stocks. short sale is sometimes a dangerous observe in day mercantilism. Some traders square measure long-biased. They exclusively acquire stocks inside the hope of commerce them higher. I don't have any bias. {i will|i will be able to|i'll} be able to short sell once I assume the setup is ready, which i will acquire whenever it fits my strategy. Having aforesaid that, i am extra careful once I short stocks. Some ways in which I justify in Chapter seven work only for long positions

Some ways in which work only for mercantilism will add every long and short positions hoping on the setup. I justify these positions well in Chapter seven.

Individual traders, like you which i, square measure referred to as retail traders. we'll be part-time traders, or full-time traders, but we're not operative for a firm and we're not managing completely different people's money. we've got an inclination to retail traders square measure atiny low share of the amount inside the market. On the other hand, there square measure Wall Street investment banks, mutual funds and hedge funds, the supposed institutional traders, and most of their mercantilism depends on refined portable computer algorithms and high frequency mercantilism. rarely is any human involved inside the day group action of these massive accounts. Through in spite of suggests that, institutional traders have sizable cash behind them which they're typically very aggressive.

You may properly raise, "How can a non-public businessperson, like you and American state, coming back later to the game, contend against institutional traders and win?" The Achilles' heel of most institutional traders is that they have to trade, whereas individual traders square measure liberal to trade or to stay out of the market as they hold best. Banks ought to move inside the market and trade large volumes of shares at nearly any value. a non-public merchant is liberal to look ahead to the foremost effective opportunities to arise.

Unfortunately, however, the majority of retail traders eat this fantastic advantage by over-trading. a non-public WHO must succeed against the giants ought to develop patience and eliminate greed. the ultimate word disadvantage of losers is not their account size but their lack of selfdiscipline, over-trading, and their unhealthy money management.

I incessantly use the analogy of retail day mercantilism and guerrilla warfare. Guerrilla warfare is associate irregular approach to warfare inside that atiny low cluster of combatants, like paramilitary personnel or armed civilians, use hit-and-run military techniques, like ambushes, sabotage, raids and petty warfare, to maneuver around a much bigger and less-mobile ancient military force. The u. s. military is taken under consideration to be one in each of the foremost formidable fighting forces within the world. However, they suffered significantly as a results of jungle warfare ways used against them in country. Earlier examples embody the eu resistance movements that fought against Reich throughout warfare a pair of.

GUERRILLA MERCANTILISM

In guerrilla mercantilism, as a result of the term suggests, you are out of sight, anticipating a chance to maneuver throughout and out of the financial jungle in an exceedingly short quantity of it slow to get quick profits whereas keeping your risk to a minimum. You don't have to be compelled to defeat or outsmart investment banks. You're simply anticipating an opportunity to achieve your daily profit target. As a retail day businessperson, you're taking advantage of volatility inside the market. If the markets square measure flat, you are not about to build any cash; exclusively high frequency traders create money to a lower place these circumstances. Therefore, you would like to go looking out stocks which will create quick moves to the upside or to the recoil throughout a relatively sure manner. Institutional traders, on the other hand, square measure commerce with very high frequency and may benefit of very little movements of import, or as a result of it's generally referred to as, from a "choppy worth action".

It is terribly important to stay off from stocks that square measure being heavily listed by institutional traders. As a non-public retail day businessperson, you wish to follow retail mercantilism territory. you will not trade stocks that completely different retail traders do not appear to be mercantilism or not seeing. The strength of retail day mercantilism ways in which is that completely different retail traders are utilizing them. the extra traders utilizing these ways in which, the higher they'll work. As extra of us acknowledge the road inside the sand, extra of us is buying at that point. This, of course, suggests that the stock will move up faster. The additional customers, the quicker it will move. this could be why many traders square measure happy to share their day mercantilism ways in which. It not exclusively helps completely different traders to become extra profitable, but it collectively can increase the amount of traders WHO square measure using these methods. there's no profit out of sight these ways in which or keeping them secret.

As a district of the recursive mercantilism by portable computer systems, the majority of the stocks will trend with the overall market unless they have a reason to not. So, if the market is moving up, the majority of stocks square measure moving up. If the overall market goes down, the prices of the majority of stocks can go down. But, remember, there will be a handful of stocks which will buck the trend of the market as a results of they have a catalyst. I call these stocks Alpha Predators. i will be able to make a case for them in Chapter four and describe some way to appreciate them. this could be what retail traders square measure checking out - that small few stocks that are becoming to be running once the markets square measure tanking, or tanking once the markets square measure running. If the market is running, and these stocks square measure running too, that is fine. {you just|you only|you merely} need to make sure {you're|you square measure} mercantilism stocks that are moving as a results of they have a elementary reason to maneuver and do not appear to be simply moving with the overall market conditions.

You may raise, what is the elemental catalyst for stocks that build them appropriate for day trading? Here square measure some examples:

- Earnings reports
- Earnings warnings/pre-announcements
- Earnings surprises
- FDA approval/disapproval
- Mergers/acquisitions
- Alliances/partnerships/major product releases
- Major contract wins/losses
- Restructuring/layoffs/management changes
- Stock splits/buybacks/debt offerings

If there is a quick dump as a results of unhealthy news, many people will notice and start observance the stock for what is referred to as a bottom reversal. If stocks square measure trending down with the overall market, like oil was it slow ago, you can not do associate honest reversal trade. Their value pops up by 10 cents, and you're thinking that it's a reversal, nevertheless they are sold-out off for a new fifty cents. They're merchandising off as a results of their trending with every the overall market and their sector. Oil was a weak sector for a brief time and conjointly the bulk of the oil and energy stocks were commerce off. once a sector is weak, that is not associate honest time for making a reversal trade. That will where have to be compelled to differentiate. thus here's the fourth rule of day trading:

Rule 4: incessantly raise, "Is this stock moving as a results of the overall market is moving, or is it moving as a results of it is a singular catalyst?" That's when you wish to try to to a small amount bit of study. As you become extra seasoned as a businessperson, you will be able to differentiate between catalyst-based value action and general market trending.

As mentioned, as a distributor, you wish to use caution simply} just do not appear to get on the incorrect side of the trade against institutional traders. but do you shut out of their way? instead of making an attempt to go looking out institutional traders, you discover out where the retail traders square measure hanging out on it day so you trade with them. place confidence in a yard for an immediate. You don't have to be compelled to be off inside the sandbox doing all of your own issue, commerce a stock that no-one is paying attention to. You're inside the incorrect place. Focus where everyone else is focused: specialise in the stock that is moving every single day and receiving just about an oversized quantity of action. That's what day traders square measure viewing. square measure you able to day trade stock like Apple or Priceline or Coca-Cola or IBM? in the end you will, but these square measure slow moving stocks that square measure dominated by institutional traders and recursive traders, and usually terms they're about to be very hard to day trade. place confidence in it as a result of the equivalent of hanging enter that isolated sandbox instead of hanging out in conjunction with your peers within the playground where the cool cats square measure.

How do you make sure what retail traders square measure targeted on and your point that playground?

There square measure a couple of of the way to catch your best place. One is by gazing day mercantilism stock scanners. The stocks that square measure gapping significantly up or down are becoming to be the stocks that retail traders square measure gazing. Secondly, it's smart to be in grips with social media and a community of traders. StockTwits and Twitter square measure generally sensible places to be told what is trending. If you follow a handful of traders, then you will be able to see for yourself what most square measure talking relating to. There's an oversized advantage to being throughout a community of traders, sort of a speak space, and there square measure several chat rooms on cyberspace. If you're commerce totally on your own, you are off inside the corner of that proverbial playground. you are not in grips with what completely different traders do, and inevitably you will build it terribly hard on yourself as a results of you will not acknowledge where the activity is. I even have tried block out social media and commerce throughout a bubble, primarily doing my terribly own issue, and it failed to work. Draw on the laws of highschool survival to guide you!

A little extra relating to what I do: As each day businessperson, I don't trade supported the company's fundamentals like product, earnings, earningsper-share growth and financial statements. I'm not a value capitalist and I'm not a prolonged term capitalist. I don't trade Future either; but I do use Futures to realize associate understanding of the overall market direction inside the near-term future. I'm collectively a swing businessperson. In swing commerce, I head to head do care greatly relating to the basics of the companies i choose to trade: their earnings, dividends, earnings-per-share, and lots of various criteria.

the majority of day traders don't trade penny stocks or on the over-the-counter (OTC) market.

Penny stocks square measure very manipulated which they do not follow any of the principles of the standard methods.

You may be surprised, but on nearly every single day inside the market, there is a stock having a large day as a results of the company has free earnings, had a bulletin, or had one factor unhealthy or smart happen to that. These square measure the fundamental catalysts that you simply ought to hunt for. what is going to my day look like as each day trader? You examine it well in big apple time, is once the market will have the foremost mercantilism volume and collectively the foremost volatility. this could be the foremost effective time to trade and to significantly specialise in momentum mercantilism (which square measure explained later). The advantage of obtaining all of that volume is that it provides liquidity. this suggests there square measure several customers and lots of sellers, that in turn means that you will merely get in and out of trades. Around mid-day, you'll need smart commerce patterns but you will not have the amount. this suggests a scarceness of liquidity, that produces it more durable to urge in and out of stocks. this could be significantly important to place confidence in if you would like to need large shares. My focus has incessantly been on commerce at the market's gap, that is 9:30 a.m. within the long island (Eastern time). I head to head trade exclusively within the first one or a pair of hours of the market's gap. If you be a part of the private website that i discussed over, you will see that I rarely build any trades once 10:30 a.m.

On associate honest day I even have reached my goal by 7:30 a.m. Vancouver time (10:30 a.m. big apple time) and I'm easing up. typically by time of day I've already hit my goal and i am about to be sitting on my hands unless there is that glorious setup. From 4 p.m. until 6 p.m.

Why is that the market at low volume throughout the mid-day and afternoon? Imagine you created $1,000 by 10 a.m. What square measure you about to do? square measure you planning to go away thereupon profit or are you able to retain commerce until you lose that money?

Hopefully you will walk off. many people square measure finished for the day at some purpose inside the morning, so they are about to go taking part in or pay the rest of the day at their leisure. But, if they have lost $1,000 by 10 a.m., those traders square measure planning to keep fighting it bent keep inside the market. they are about to keep commerce, attempting to make back what they lost. this implies that mid-day commerce is dominated by traders WHO have lost inside the morning and square measure sharply making an attempt to regain their losses. That causes tons of volatility, and not throughout an excellent means. That causes stocks to extend and down as a results of of us are becoming into and out with market orders. It's currently of day that I concede to be dominated by extra amateur traders and mercantilism. Extrapolating from this, I'm going terribly simple at mid-day. I avoid pre-market mercantilism as a results of there's a awfully low liquidity as there square measure only a few traders mercantilism. which implies stocks can occur a dollar, then drop a dollar, and you can't get in and out with large shares. you have got need to travel terribly little, and you have got to use such little positions that, on behalf of ME a minimum of, it's merely not worthy. If you do not mind mercantilism in just a couple of of hundred shares, then you will undoubtedly trade pre-market.

I board Vancouver, Canada, therefore in my zone the market opens at 6:30 a.m. (Pacific time). this suggests that my days begin terribly early. the great advantage on behalf of me is that I square measure typically finished mercantilism before most of the oldsters in my city square measure even out of bed. i will be able to then pay the rest of my day athletics, climbing, with family and friends, or specializing in numerous work and conjointly the opposite businesses that I even have. I try to hit my daily goal by 7:30 a.m. my time (which is 10:30 a.m. jap time) so ease up. you acknowledge but easy it's to lose money. Once you have got some benefit your pocket, you got to hold on to that.

To be a winning day merchant, you would like to master three essential components of trading: sound subject, a series of logical mercantilism ways in which, and a good risk management originated. These square measure a bit like the three legs of a stool - take away one and conjointly the stool will fall. It's a typical beginner's mistake to focus solely on indicators and mercantilism ways in which.

A good mercantilism strategy delivers positive expectancy; it generates larger profits than losses over associate quantity of it slow. But, detain mind, even the foremost strictly dead strategy does not guarantee success in each trade. No strategy can assure you of never having a losing trade or maybe suffering a series of losing trades. this could be why risk management ought to be a significant a part of every mercantilism strategy.

The inability to manage losses is that the darling reason that new traders fail in day mercantilism. It's a regular human inclination to easily settle for profits quickly and in addition to need to attend until losing trades come back to even. By the time some new traders learn to manage their risk, their accounts square measure badly, if not irreparably, damaged.

To be a winning merchant, you wish to find out risk management rules so firmly implement them. you wish to own a line inside the sand that tells you once to urge out of the trade. It's about to be necessary from time to time to provide in and say, "I was wrong," or "The setup isn't ready nonetheless," or "I'm getting out of the style." I'm typically a winning merchant, but I still lose ofttimes. which implies i want to own found the best thanks to be a really sensible loser. Lose gracefully. Take the losses and go away.

I can't emphasize enough but important it's to be associate honest loser. you have to be able to accept a loss. It's associate integral a district of day mercantilism. altogether of the ways in which I justify in Chapter seven, I'll permit you to know what is my entry purpose, my exit target, furthermore as my stop loss. you need to follow the foundations and plans of your strategy, associated this could be one in each of the challenges you will face when you're in an extremely dangerous trade. you will very likely understand yourself justifying staying in associate extremely dangerous trade by speech, "Well, you know, it's Apple, and that they produce very nice smartphones. they are without doubt not going out of business. i am going to merely hold this barely longer."

You do not have to be compelled to try and that. you wish to follow the foundations of your strategy. you'll be able to perpetually come back in, but it's arduous to measure through a large loss. You'll suppose, "I do not have to be compelled to need a $50 loss." Well, you actually do not have to be compelled to need a future $200 loss. And if you complete up taking $800 loss, it would be extremely arduous to measure through that. Take the short losses, get out, and square measure out there back once the temporal property is best.

Every time you trade, you're exposing yourself to the danger of losing money. however does one minimize that risk? you would like to hunt out associate honest setup and manage the danger with correct share size and stop loss.

Here is my next rule:

Rule 5: Success in day mercantilism comes from risk management - finding low-risk entries with a high potential reward. The minimum win: lose magnitude relation on behalf of ME is 2:1. an honest setup could be a probability for you to urge into a trade with as little risk as attainable. which implies you'd probably be risking $100; but you have the potential to create $300. You'd call that a 3 to at least one profit-to-loss magnitude relation. On the other hand, if you get into a setup where you are risking $100 to make $10, you have a one risk-reward magnitude relation, and that is about to be a trade simply} just mustn't take. sensible traders will not take trades with profit-to-loss ratios of however a try of to at least one. It means that if you buy $1,000 value of stock, and square measure risking $100 on it, you need to sell it for a minimum of $1,200 therefore you will produce a minimum of $200. Of course, if the worth comes all the means all the way down to $900, you wish to accept the loss and exit the trade with exclusively $900 ($100 loss).

If you cannot understand a setup with associate honest profit-to-loss magnitude relation, then you got to go on and keep checking out another trade. As a bargainer, you are invariably checking out opportunities to urge low risk entries with huge win potential. Having the power to identify setups that have huge win potential is in addition a district of the tutorial methodology. As a beginner bargainer you will not be able to differentiate between an expansion of setups. {it may|it's planning to|it should} be robust for you to acknowledge what is a homerun Bull Flag and what's going to find yourself being a "false breakout". That's one factor that comes with every expertise and training. we have a tendency to square measure planning to cowl this in extra depth inside the approaching back chapters. Using a a try of to at least one win:lose magnitude relation, i'll be wrong fourhundredth of the time and still produce cash. Again, your job as daily merchant is managing risk; it is not buying and merchandising stocks. Your broker is buying and selling stocks for you inside the market.

FINDING THE RIGHT STOCKS FOR DAY MERCANTILISM

Your job is to manage your risk and account. Whenever you click "buy" in your mercantilism platform, you expose your money to a risk. however do you manage that? You essentially have three steps in managing risk. you wish to boost yourself:

This Chapter focuses on finding the right stocks for day mercantilism. i am going to justify well the thanks to understand stocks that square measure applicable for day mercantilism and what criteria you ought to explore for in them. you wish to avoid stocks that (1) square measure heavily listed by computers and institutional traders, (2) have very little relative mercantilism volume, (3) square measure penny stocks that square measure very manipulated, and (4) don't have any reason to maneuver (no basic catalysts). i am going to justify these in extra detail in Chapter four.

Do bear in mind that risk management starts from choosing the right reasonably stock to trade. You'll be able to have the best platform and tools and be a master of how, however if you are mercantilism the wrong stock, you will without doubt lose money.

One share, 10 shares or 100 shares? What relating to one thousand shares? This depends on your account size and your daily target. If you are targeting $1,000 a day, then ten or twenty shares might not be enough. You either need to be compelled to require loads of shares or increase your account size. If you don't have enough money to trade for a $1,000 daily target, you got to lower your daily goal.

I am holding around $25,000 in my mercantilism account which i generally choose 800 shares to trade. My daily goal is $500 or $120,000/year. That's ample for my fashion. What's your mercantilism goal?

The absolute most a bargainer got to risk on any trade could be a try of of his or her account equity. as associate example, if you have a $30,000 account, you got to not risk over $600 per trade, and if you have a $10,000 account, you got to not risk over $200. If your account is small, limit yourself to mercantilism fewer shares. If you see a fairly trade, but a logical stop would need to be compelled to be placed where over a try of your money would be at risk, then die that trade and look for an additional one. you will be able to risk less, but you got to never risk loads of. you need to avoid risking over a try of on a trade.

Risk Management

Step 1: make sure your most dollar risk for the trade you're planning (never over a try of of your account). Calculate this before your mercantilism day starts.

Step 2: Estimate your most risk per share, the strategy stop loss, in dollars, from your entry.

Step 3: Divide "1" by "2" to hunt out completely the foremost style of shares you're allowed to trade once.

For example, if you have a $40,000 account, the 2 rule will limit your risk on any trade to $800. Let's assume you would like to be conservative and risk only 1 of that account, or $400. which will be the 1st step.

Suppose you concentrate on the stock of BlackBerry (ticker: BBRY) for ABCD Pattern Strategy. you buy the stock at $16 and need to sell it at $19, with a stop loss at $14.50. You'll be risking $1.50 per share. which will be the Step a try of risk management.

For Step 3, calculate your share size by dividing "Step 1" by "Step 2" to hunt out the utmost size you will trade. throughout this instance, you will be allowed to buy for exclusively 266 shares (or rounded to 250 shares). With the ways in which introduced in Chapter seven, I justify where my stop loss would be supported technical analysis and my trade originated. I cannot ponder most loss for your account as a results of I in the end don't perceive your account size. you wish to make that judgment for yourself. as associate example, once your stop would be higher than of a moving average, you would like to calculate and see if that stop would be larger than your most account size or not. If break of moving average will yield a $600 loss, and you have got set a $400 most loss per trade, then you ought to either take fewer shares in this trade or not take that exchange the slightest degree and watch for another probability.

You may properly argue that it will be robust to calculate share size or stop loss supported a most loss on your account whereas you are waiting to leap into a trade. you will got to produce a decision fast instead you may lose the chance. I understand that scheming your stop loss associated most loss in your account size in an extremely live trade is hard. Bear in mind Rule 1? Day mercantilism isn't speculated to be easy. mercantilism needs apply which i powerfully recommend that new traders paper trade to a lower place direction for a minimum of three months in associate extremely live simulated account. It sounds crazy at the beginning, but you will quickly learn the way to manage your account and your risk per trade. {you may|you'll|you can} be surprised at but quickly the human brain will do calculations on what share size to need and where to line the stop loss.

A burning question when you start your mercantilism career is "Why do most traders fail?"

Day mercantilism desires you to make quick selections and at constant time to be terribly disciplined. when you hear breaking news that associate activist capitalist has merely taken a stake in Amazon.com Inc., your initial reaction would be to load the boat. i will be able to hear the logic that compels you. "Let's acquire 5 thousand shares in Amazon! Let's placed on a large order!" but you would like to be able to produce a quick turn whether or not you got to acquire or sell or sell short that stock, and you would like to make that decision with discipline.

My mercantilism ways in which slowly improved with time, but the breakthrough came once I completed that the key to winning was dominant myself and active self-discipline. it's arduous enough to understand what the market will do, however if you don't perceive what you will do, the game is lost. New mercantilism ways in which, tips from ME or from this book, or maybe the foremost refined software package believable, won't facilitate traders WHO cannot handle themselves.

You must raise yourself questions:

- Does this match into my mercantilism strategy?
- What methods will this match into?
- If this trade goes the wrong manner, where is my stop?
- How abundant money am I risking inside the trade, and what is the reward potential?

This is what many traders understand robust. All of these selections, the very methodology of creating positive these selections match into your risk tolerance and your strategy parameters, square measure a difficult multitasking call. Not exclusively is it multitasking, however it's multitasking whereas to a lower place stress.

I understand that stress. There square measure times once i have been inside the trade, had $15,000 in shares, and each one I needed to do to to was sell. but as i wont to be observation my keyboard, I couldn't even estimate that keys to punch. this sort of palsy isn't uncommon once you're inundated. Whenever that happens, you would like to appreciate simply} just have pushed yourself barely too solution of your temperature. It happens {to each|to each} single one in every of u. s.. Expect it to. Once you have some experience beneath your belt, it's sensible to work on the sting of your temperature therefore you are perpetually pushing your boundaries. However, if you discover yourself too means outside of your temperature and out of doors of your risk tolerance, you will be able to end up making some important and overpriced mistakes.

I encourage you to foster a state of awareness within yourself. Dial in:

- Are you focused?

- Are you calm?

- Are you making sensible decisions?

- Be in grips with the results of your selections and constantly be reviewing your performance.

- square measure you mercantilism profitably?

Have you had five winners {in a|during a|in an extremely|in a very}n exceedingly row or have you ever ever had 5 losses in a row?

If you are on a streak, are you able to be in grips in conjunction with your own emotions and maintain your calm, or are you able to let your judgment? I cannot amplify but vital that talent square measure planning to be. contemplate talent and discipline to be your mercantilism muscles. Muscles want exercise to grow and, once you've mature them, they need to be exercised otherwise you may lose them. that is what I experience every day: often sweat my ability to use self-control and discipline. a number of these skills, however, square measure almost like learning to ride a bicycle. Once you've learned it, riding a motorcycle can be a talent that can't be got rid of. Once you've learned it, the talent of distinctive associate honest stock chart isn't about to escape. however bear in mind, discipline could be a few stuff you got to constantly work to be a booming merchant. You've entered a profession inside that you will invariably be learning. That's nice. In fact, it's over nice - it's stimulating. but it is vital to remember that if you start to urge over-confident and suppose you've outsmarted the market on mercantilism data, or simply} just ought to not learn to any extent further, you'll typically get a quick reminder from that market. You'll lose money and you may see that the market is correcting you. i will be able to reiterate: having the power to make quick selections and having the ability to create and so follow your mercantilism rules square measure vital for accomplishment inside the market. As you continue through this book, you are about to scan loads of relating to risk management.

Everything that traders do comes back to risk management as a results of ultimately it's the foremost vital thought for a bargainer to grasp. All day long, you're managing risk. related to could} be the ability to manage risk so as that you simply may produce sensible selections - even inside the warmth of the moment. That's following rule of day trading: Rule 6: Your broker will acquire and sell stocks for you. Your exclusively job as daily bargainer is to manage risk. you cannot be a booming day bargainer whereas not wonderful risk management skills, though you are the master of the numerous effective ways in which

As mentioned before, traders square measure inside the business of mercantilism. you would like to stipulate your risk as a business person - the utmost amount of money you'll risk on any single trade. Sadly, there isn't any customary dollar amount that i will be able to recommend. As explained earlier, an appropriate risk depends on the size of your mercantilism account furthermore as on your mercantilism technique, temperament and risk tolerance. but bear in mind the 2 rule explained on prime of. it's value repeating: absolutely the most traders might risk on any trade could be a try of their account equity. as an example, if you have a $30,000 account, you will not risk over $600 per trade, and if you have a $10,000 account, you will not risk over $200. If your account is small, limit yourself to mercantilism fewer shares. If you see a lovely trade, but a logical stop would need to be compelled to be placed where over a try of your equity would be at risk, die that trade and look for a further trade. you will risk less, but you will never risk loads of. you wish to avoid risking loads of than a try of on a trade.

The following square measure several basic mercantilism ways by that day traders conceive to produce profits. in addition, some day traders in addition use capitalist finance ways (more commonly seen in recursive trading) to trade specifically against irrational behavior from day traders using the approaches below. It's necessary for a businessperson to remain versatile and alter techniques to match dynamical market conditions. a number of these approaches want mercantilism stocks; the businessperson borrows stock from his broker and sells the borrowed stock, hoping that the worth will fall and he square measure able to purchase the shares at a lower value, thus keeping the excellence as their profit. There square measure several technical problems with short sales - the broker won't have shares to lend throughout a particular issue, the broker can want the come back of its shares at any time, and a couple of restrictions square measure obligatory in America by the U.S. Securities and Exchange Commission on short-selling. variety of those restrictions (in specific the dealings rule) do not apply to trades of stocks that are actually shares of exchange-traded fund (ETF).

Trend following, a way used all told mercantilism time-frames, assumes that cash instruments that square measure rising steady will still rise, and therefore the alternative means around with falling. The trend follower buys associate instrument that has been rising, or short sells a falling one, inside the expectation that the trend will continue. Trend following or trend commerce is also a mercantilism strategy in line therewith one can purchase associate quality once its value trend goes up, and sell once its trend goes down, expecting value movements to continue.

There square measure style of numerous techniques, calculations and time-frames which is able to be accustomed make sure the ultimate direction of the market to return up with a trade signal (forex signals), along side this worth calculation, moving averages and channel breakouts. Traders WHO use this strategy do not aim to forecast or predict specific value levels; they simply mount the trend and ride it attributable to the varied techniques and time frames employed by trend followers to identify trends, trend followers as a bunch do not appear to be constantly powerfully associated with one another. Trend following is used by physical object commerce advisors (CTAs) as a result of the predominant strategy of technical traders. Analysis done by expert Burghardt has shown that between 2000-2009 there was a awfully high correlation (.97) between trend following CTAs and conjointly the broader CTA index.

Trend following is associate investment or commerce strategy that tries to need advantage of long, medium and/or short moves that seem to play enter various markets. Traders WHO use a trend following strategy do not aim to forecast or predict specific value levels; they simply mount the trend (when they perceived that a trend has established with their own peculiar reasons or rules) and ride it. The argument can also be created that trend traders do thus forecast the long-term direction of prices, i.e. that this trend will continue. These traders commonly enter inside the market once the trend "properly" establishes itself, indulgent that the trend will persist for associate extended time, and for this reason they antedate the initial turning purpose profit. A market "trend" is also an inclination of a cash worth to maneuver in associate extremely express direction over time. this could be typically explained by as an example the result where investors square measure triggered to follow different investors. If there is a flip contrary to the trend, they exit and wait until the flip establishes itself as a trend inside the opposite means. simply just in case their rules signal associate exit, the traders exit but enters once the trend re-establishes.

Cutting Loss. Exit market once market flip against them to attenuate losses, and "let the profits run", once the market trend goes patently until the market exhausted and reverses to book profit. Commonly, a trend reversal once associate extended profitable trade is termed a "give-back" loss whereas trend reversals in vary sure markets square measure typically cited as a "whipsaw" loss. This mercantilism or "betting with positive edge" methodology involves a risk management half that uses three elements: style of shares or futures management, this value, and current market volatility. associate initial risk rule determines position size at time of entry. Specifically what proportion to buy for or sell depends on the scale of the mercantilism account and conjointly the volatility of the issue. Changes in value would possibly cause a gradual reduction or an increase of the initial trade. On the other hand, adverse value movements would possibly cause associate exit from the entire trade.

In the words of Tom Basso, inside the book Trade Your because of cash Freedom:

"Let's break down the term Trend Following into its parts. the first [*fr1] is "trend". every dealer needs a trend to make money. If you're thinking that that relating to it, however what the technique, if there is not a trend once you purchase, then you will not be able to sell at higher prices..."Following" is that following a district of the term. we've got an inclination to use this word as a results of trend followers constantly anticipate the trend to shift first, then "follow" it. "

The key reasons for trending markets square measure style of activity biases that cause market participants to over-react:

Herding: once markets have trended, some traders mount the bandwagon, so prolonging the gregarious result and trends.

Confirmation Bias: people tend to look for information that confirm their views and beliefs. this might lead investors to buy for assets that have recently created money, and sell assets that have declined, inflicting trends to continue.

RISK MANAGEMENT

Some risk-management models will sell in down markets as, as associate example, some risk budgets square measure broken, and replenish markets as new risk budgets square measure unbarred, inflicting trends to persist.

- Price: one in every of the first rules of trend following is that value is that the most concern. Traders would possibly use different indicators showing where value might go next or what it got to be but as a general rule these ought to be ignored. A businessperson need exclusively be distressed relating to what the market is doing, not what the market might do. this value and exclusively the price tells you what the market is doing

- Money management: Another determinative of trend following is not the temporal property of the trade or the indicator, but rather the selection of what proportion to trade over the course of the trend.

- Risk control: Cut losses is that the rule. this implies that in periods of higher market volatility, the commerce size is reduced. Throughout losing periods, positions square measure reduced and trade size is decrease. the foremost objective is to preserve capital until loads of positive value trends seem.

- Rules: Trend following got to be systematic. value and time square measure vital the smallest amount bit times. this technique is not supported academic degree analysis of basic give and demand factors.
- Diversification: analysis written by hedge fund manager Andreas Clenow shows that cross quality diversification is a crucial a district of trained trend following.

Example

A monger would confirm a security to trade

(currencies/commodities/financials) and would come back up with a preliminary strategy, such as:

Commodity: oil

Trading approach: long and short alternately.

Entrance: once the fifty quantity simple moving average (SMA) crosses over the 100 amount SMA, go long once the market opens. The crossover suggests that the trend has recently turned up.

Exit: Exit long and go short resulting day once 100 quantity SMA crosses over fifty amount SMA. The crossover suggests that the trend has turned down.

Stop loss: Set a stop loss supported most loss acceptable. as associate example, if the recent, say 10-day, average true vary is zero.5% of current worth, stop loss is set at 4x0.5% = 2%. typical data on stop losses set the danger per trade anywhere between 1%-5% of capital for one trade; this risk varies from one monger to a unique.

The monger would then backtest the strategy, practice actual info and would appraise the strategy. The machine would generate countable style of trades, the fraction of winning/losing trades, average profit/loss, average holding time, most drawdown, and conjointly the profit/loss. The monger can then experiment and refine the strategy. Care ought to be taken, however, to avoid over-optimization.

It is possible that a majority of the trades is additionally unprofitable, but by "cutting the losses" and "letting profits run", the overall strategy is additionally profitable. Trend mercantilism is just for a market that is quiet (relative low volatility) and trending. For this reason, trend traders typically think about commodities, that show a stronger tendency to trend than on stocks, that square measure loads of likely to be mean reverting (which favors swing traders).

In addition to quiet low volatility markets, where trend following ways in which perform well, trend commerce is in addition very effective in high volatility markets (market crash). Trend traders "short" the market and just like the disadvantage market trend.

In finance, associate electronic mercantilism platform in addition known as a web mercantilism platform can be a computer computer code package program which will be used to place orders for financial product over a network with a money intercessor. Varied cash merchandise is listed by the mercantilism platform, over a communication network with a cash intercessor or directly between the participants or members of the mercantilism platform. This includes merchandise like stocks, bonds, currencies, commodities, derivatives et al., with a cash intercessor, like brokers, market makers, Investment banks or stock exchanges. Such platforms allow electronic mercantilism to be assigned by users from any location and square measure in distinction to ancient floor mercantilism by using open outcry and phone based totally mercantilism. generally the term mercantilism platform is in addition utilised in relation to the mercantilism computer code package alone.

Electronic mercantilism platforms usually stream live market prices on those users can trade and can provide further mercantilism tools, like charting packages, news feeds and account management functions. Some platforms square measure specifically designed to allow folks to realize access to cash markets that will erstwhile exclusively be accessed by specialist mercantilism firms. they'll even be designed to automatically trade specific ways supported technical analysis or to do and do high-frequency mercantilism.

Algorithmic mercantilism can be a technique of execution orders using machine-controlled pre-programmed mercantilism directions accounting for variables like time, price, and volume to send very little slices of the order (child orders) resolute the market over time. They were developed thus traders haven't got to be compelled to constantly watch a stock and repeatedly send those slices out manually commonplace "algos" embrace proportion of Volume, Pegged, VWAP, TWAP, and Implementation deficit, Target shut. inside the ordinal century, algorithmic mercantilism has been gaining traction with every retail and institutional traders. it's wide utilised by investment banks, pension funds, mutual funds, and hedge funds as a results of these institutional traders need to be compelled to execute huge orders in markets that cannot support all of the size quickly.

The term is in addition used to mean machine-controlled mercantilism system. These do thus have the goal of constructing a profit in addition known as equipment mercantilism, Quant or Quantitative mercantilism, these embrace mercantilism ways that square measure heavily keen about difficult mathematical formulas and high-speed computer programs.

Such systems run ways along side market making, inter-market spreading, arbitrage, or pure speculation like trend following. many conjure the category of high-frequency mercantilism (HFT), that square measure defined by high turnover and high order-to-trade ratios. As a result, in Feb 2012, the products Futures mercantilism Commission (CFTC) formed a special unit that coarctate academics and business specialists to advise the CFTC on but best to stipulate HFT. HFT ways utilize computers that make elaborate selections to initiate orders supported information that is received electronically, before human traders square measure capable of method the data they observe. algorithmic mercantilism associated HFT have resulted in an extremely dramatic modification of the market microstructure, notably inside the means that liquidity is provided

Stock market cycles square measure the semi-permanent worth patterns of stock markets and square measure generally associated with general business cycles. they are key to technical analysis where the approach to finance is based on cycles or continuation worth patterns. The effectiveness of the foreshadowing nature of these cycles is moot and a couple of of those cycles square measure quantitatively examined for maths significance.

Well known cycles include:

- The satellite cycle

- Annual seasonality, conjointly known as Sell in would possibly or the Hallowe'en indicator still as a result of the Jan result and New Style calendar month impact.

- The four-year North American nation presidential election cycle inside the America.

- The 17.6 Year stock market Cycle.

- The sixty year Kondratiev cycles

Investment advisor Mark Hulbert has tracked the long-run performance of Norman Fosback's a Seasonality temporal property System that mixes month-end and holiday-based buy/sell rules. per Hulbert, this methodology has been able to trounce the market with significantly less risk per Stan Weinstein there square measure four stages in associate extremely major cycle of stocks, stock sectors or the stock market as a whole. These four stages square measure (1) consolidation or base building (2) upward advancement (3) conclusion (4) decline.

Cyclical cycles generally last four years, with bull and industry phases lasting 1–3 years, whereas lay cycles last regarding thirty years with bull and industry phases lasting 10–20 years. it's generally accepted[citation needed] that in early 2011 the America stock market is in associate extremely circular bull section as a result of it's been moving up for style of years. It's in addition generally accepted[citation needed] that it's in associate extremely lay bear section as a result of it's been stagnant since the stock market peak in 2000. The long run Kondratiev cycles square measure a pair of lay cycles long and last roughly sixty years. The tip of the Kondratiev cycle is amid economic troubles, just like the initial depression of the decade, the great Depression of the Thirties and so the present nice Recession.

The presence of multiple cycles of varied periods and magnitudes in conjunction with linear trends, can create to difficult patterns, that square measure mathematically generated through analysis.

In order for associate capitalist to extra merely visualise a extended term cycle (or a trend), he generally will place a shorter term cycle sort of a moving average on prime of it.

A common scan of a stock market pattern is one that involves a specific timeframe (for example a 6-month chart with daily worth intervals). throughout this moderately a chart one would possibly manufacture and observe any of the next trends or trend relationships:

- A semi-permanent trend, which may appear as linear
- Intermediate term trends and their relationship to the long-run trend

Random worth movements or consolidation (sometimes discovered as 'noise') and its relationship to a minimum of one in all the upper than as an example, if one look at a extended timeframe (perhaps a 2-year chart with weekly worth intervals), this trend may appear as a locality of a much bigger cycle (primary trend). modification to a shorter timeframe (such as a 10-day chart by using 60-minute worth intervals), would possibly reveal worth movements that appear as shorter-term trends in distinction to the primary trend on the sixmonth, daily amount, chart.

CONTRARIAN FINANCE

Contrarian finance is associate investment strategy that is defined by obtaining and mercantilism in distinction to the prevailing sentiment of the time. associate capitalist believes that positive crowd behavior among investors can lead to exploitable mispricing in securities markets. as associate example, widespread pessimism a handful of stock can drive a value so low that it overstates the company's risks, and understates its prospects for returning to profit. distinctive and shopping for such distressed stocks, and mercantilism them once the company recovers, can lead to above-average gains. Conversely, widespread optimism might lead to inexcusably high valuations which will eventually lead to drops, once those high expectations do not pan out. Avoiding (or short-selling) investments in over-hyped investments cut back the danger of such drops. These general principles can apply whether or not or not the investment in question could be a personal stock, associate trade sector, or a full market or the opposite quality class.

Some contrarians have a permanent market scan, whereas the majority of investors stake the market thickening. However, a capitalist does not basically have a negative scan of the overall exchange, nor do they have to believe that it's forever overvalued, or that the normal data is commonly wrong. Rather, a capitalist seeks opportunities to buy for or sell specific investments once the majority of investors appear to be doing the opposite, to the aim where that investment has become mispriced. Whereas extra "buy" candidates square measure most likely to be celebrated throughout market declines (and vice versa), these opportunities can occur in periods once the overall market is sometimes rising or falling.

Contrarian finance is expounded to cost finance during this the capitalist is in addition attempting to seek out mispriced investments and buying those that appear to be undervalued by the market. inside the bible on capitalist thinking, "The Art of Contrary Thinking" (1954) by Humphrey B. Neill, he notes it's easy to hunt out one factor to travel contrary to, but hard to seek out once everybody believes it. He concludes "when everybody thinks alike, everyone seems to be likely to be wrong." Some wellknown value investors like John Neff have questioned whether or not or not there is such issue as a "contrarian", seeing it as primarily similar with value finance. One potential distinction is that a value stock, in finance theory, is also celebrated by financial metrics just like the worth or P/E ratio. A capitalist capitalist might contemplate those metrics, but is in addition fascinated by measures of "sentiment" regarding the stock among completely different investors, like sell-side analyst coverage and earnings forecasts, mercantilism volume, and media comment relating to the company and its business prospects.

In the example of a stock that has born due to excessive pessimism, one can see similarities to the "margin of safety" that value capitalist Benjamin Graham wished once obtaining stocks—essentially, having the power to buy for shares at a discount to their intrinsic value.

Arguably, that margin of safety is extra most likely to exist once a stock has fallen an honest deal, that variety of drop is typically within the interior of negative news and general pessimism.

Along with this, tho' extra dangerous, is shorting overvalued stocks. This want 'deep pockets' during this associate overvalued security might still rise, because of over-optimism, for quite it slow. Eventually, the short-seller believes, the stock will 'crash and burn'.

Range mercantilism, or range-bound mercantilism, can be a commerce vogue throughout that stocks square measure watched that have either been rising off a support value or drop-off a resistance value. That is, on each occasion the stock hits a high, it falls back to the low, and contrariwise. Such a stock is speculated to be "trading throughout a range", that's that the other of trending. The vary bargainer therefore buys the stock at or on the point of the low value, and sells (and presumptively short sells) at the high. A connected approach to vary commerce is checking out moves outside of a old vary, referred to as a breakout (price moves up) or a breakdown (price moves down), and assume that when the terribly has been broken prices will continue in this direction for a couple of time.

Swing commerce can be a speculative mercantilism strategy in financial markets where a tradable and is command for between one and variety of alternative days in an attempt to learn from value changes or 'swings'. A swing commerce position is sometimes command longer than day after day mercantilism position, but shorter than get and hold investment ways in which is also command for months or years. Profits is also soughtafter by either buying associate and or mercantilism. Momentum signals (e.g., 52-week high/low) square measure shown to be used by financial analysts in their get and sell recommendations which will be applied in swing commerce.

Using a set of mathematically based objective rules for getting and selling can be a standard technique for swing traders to eliminate the judgment, emotional aspects, and labour-intensive analysis of swing commerce. The commerce rules is also used to manufacture a mercantilism rule or "trading system" by using technical analysis or basic analysis to administer get and sell signals.

Simpler rule-based commerce approaches embrace Alexander Elder's strategy, that measures the behavior of associate instrument's value trend by using three utterly completely different moving averages of closing prices. The instrument is solely listed long once the three averages square measure aligned in associate upward direction, and exclusively listed Short once the three averages square measure moving downward. commerce algorithms/systems might lose their profit potential once they acquire enough of a mass following to curtail their effectiveness: "Now it's associate race. Most square measure building extra refined algorithms, and so the extra competition exists, the smaller the profits," observes Apostle Lo, the Director of the Laboratory For financial Engineering, for the Massachusetts Institute of Technology.

Identifying once to enter and once to exit a trade is that the first challenge for all swing commerce ways in which. However, swing traders do not would love glorious timing—to support the very bottom and sell at the terribly prime of value oscillations—to build a profit. little consistent earnings that involve strict money management rules can compound returns over time.

it's generally understood[by whom?] that mathematical models and algorithms do not work for every instrument or market state of affairs.

Scalping is that the shortest time frame in commerce and it exploits very little changes in currency prices. Scalpers plan to act like ancient market makers or specialists. to create the unfold implies that to buy for at {the value|the worth|the value} and sell at the raise price, thus on attain the bid/ask distinction. This procedure permits for profit even once the bid and lift do not move in any respect, as long as there square measure traders WHO square measure willing to need market prices. It commonly involves establishing and liquidating a grip quickly, generally within minutes or maybe seconds. The role of a plunger is really the role of market makers or specialists WHO square measure to stay up the liquidity and order flow of a product of a market.

The profit for each act depends exclusively on several bips (basis points), so scalping is commonly conducted once there square measure huge amounts of capital and high leverage or there square measure currency pairs where the bid-offer unfolds is slender.

Principles

Spreads square measure bonuses conjointly as costs - Stock Markets operate a bid and lift based totally system. The numerical distinction between the bid and lift prices is mentioned as a result of the unfold between them. The raise prices square measure immediate execution (market) costs for quick patrons (ask takers); bid costs for fast sellers (bid takers). If a trade is dead at market prices, closing that trade straightaway whereas not queuing would not get you back the quantity paid because of the bid/ask distinction. The unfold are viewed as commerce bonuses or costs in step with utterly completely different parties and other ways. On one hand, traders WHO do not would love to queue their order, instead paying the worth, pay the spreads (costs). On the other hand, traders WHO would love to queue and expect execution receive the spreads (bonuses). Some day commerce ways in which plan to capture the unfold as further, or maybe the only, profits for triple-crown trades.

Lower exposure, lower risks - Scalpers square measure exclusively exposed throughout a relatively short quantity, as they're doing not hold positions long. as a result of the quantity one holds decreases, the probabilities of running into extreme adverse movements, inflicting Brobdingnagian losses, decreases.

Smaller moves, easier to induce - A modification in value results from imbalance of buying and mercantilism powers. Most of the time within day after day, prices keep stable, moving within atiny low vary. this implies neither buying nor mercantilism power management true. There square measure exclusively persistently that value moves towards one direction, i.e. either buying or mercantilism power controls true. It desires larger imbalances for larger value changes. it's what scalpers probe for - capturing smaller moves that happen most of the time, as against larger ones.

Large volume, adding profits up - Since the profit obtained per share or contract is very very little because of its target of unfold, they need to trade huge thus on feature up the profits. Scalping is not applicable for massive-capital traders seeking to maneuver massive volumes quickly, apart from small-capital traders seeking to maneuver smaller volumes extra typically.

DIFFERENT PARTIES AND SPREADS

Whenever the unfold is formed one (or more) party ought to pay it (paying {the worth | the worth} to receive some value on finishing the act quickly) and a couple of party (or parties) will receive that cash as profit.

Who pays the spreads (costs)

The following traders pay the spreads:

- Momentum traders on technicals - These traders probe for fast movements hinted from quotes, prices and volumes, charts. once a real breakout happens, value becomes volatile. A unforeseen rise

- or fall would possibly occur within any second. they need to induce in quick before the price moves out of all-time low.

- Momentum traders on news - once news breaks out, the price becomes very volatile as several people gazing the news will react at extra or less identical time. A monger has got to take the market prices straightaway as a result of the possibility would possibly vanish once a second roughly.

Cut losses on values - The unfold becomes a value if the price moves against the expected direction and conjointly the monger needs to cut losses straightaway on value.

Who receives the spreads (bonuses)

The following traders receive the spreads:

- Individual scalpers - They trade for spreads and may need the advantage of larger spreads.

- Market makers and specialists - those who provide liquidity place their orders on their market books. Over the course of 1 day, a market maker would possibly fill orders for several thousands or unnumerable shares.

Spot interchange (exchanges of foreign currencies) brokers - they're doing not charge any commissions as a results of they produce profits from the bid/ask unfold quotes. On July 10, 2006, the speed between unit of measurement and North American nation dollar is one.2733 at 15:45. the inner (inter-bank dealers) bid/ask value is one.2732-5/1.2733-5. however the interchange brokers or middlemen will not offer identical competitive prices to their purchasers.

Instead they provide their own version of bid and lift quotes, say 1.2731/1.2734, of that their commissions square measure already "hidden" in it.additional competitive brokers do not charge quite an try of pips unfold on a currency where the interbank market contains a 1 pip unfold, and a couple of offer over this by quoting prices in fractional pips.

Liquidity - The liquidity of a market affects the performance of scalping.

Every product within the market receives utterly completely different unfold, because of quality differentials. the extra liquid the markets and conjointly the merchandise square measure, the tighter the spreads square measure. Some scalpers choose to exchange a extra liquid market since they'll move in and out of giant positions merely whereas not adverse market impact. completely different scalpers choose to exchange less liquid markets, that usually have significantly larger bid-ask spreads. Whereas a plunger throughout a very liquid market (for example, a market maintaining a one-penny spread) would possibly break,000 shares to create a 3 cent gain ($300), a plunger in associate illiquid market (for example, a market with a twenty 5 cent spread) would possibly pause hundred shares for a sixty cent gain ($300). Whereas there is in theory extra profit potential throughout a liquid market, it's in addition a "poker game" with additional trained players which could produce it more durable to anticipate future value action.

Volatility - in distinction to momentum traders, scalpers like stable or silent product. Imagine if it's value does not move all day, scalpers can profit all day simply by inserting their orders on identical bid and lift, making a full bunch or thousands of trades. they're doing not need to be compelled to fret relating to unforeseen value changes.

Time frame - Scalpers operate a awfully short time frame, desirous to benefit on market waves that square measure usually deficient to be seen even on the one-minute chart. This maximizes the amount of moves throughout the day that the plunger can use to create a profit.

Risk management - rather than attempting to seek out one huge trade, the tactic a trend monger may, the plunger look for several very little profits throughout the day. throughout this methodology the plunger might in addition take several very little losses throughout identical amount. For this reason a plunger ought to have very strict risk management never allowing a loss to accumulate.

Restrictions - inside the moral context speculative practices like scalping square measure thought of negatively associated to be avoided by each individual WHO conversely got to maintain an extended term horizon avoiding any sorts of short term speculation.

Rebate commerce is associate equity mercantilism vogue that uses ECN rebates as a primary offer of profit and revenue. Most ECNs charge commissions to customers WHO want to possess their orders stuffed sort of a shot at the best prices on the market, but the ECNs pay commissions to customers or sellers WHO "add liquidity" by putt limit orders that create "market-making" in associate extremely security. Rebate traders get to create money from these rebates and may generally maximize their returns by commerce low priced, high volume stocks. this enables them to trade loads of shares and contribute additional liquidity with a gaggle amount of capital, whereas limiting the danger that they're going to not be able to exit a grip inside the stock.

News collaborating in.The basic strategy of reports collaborating in is to buy for a stock that has merely declared good news or short sell on dangerous news. Such events provide large volatility in associate extremely stock and therefore the most effective chance for quick profits (or losses). determinant whether or not or not news is "good" or "bad" ought to be determined by the price action of the stock, as a results of the market reaction won't match the tone of the news itself. usually|this will be} often as a results of rumors or estimates of the event (like those issued by market and trade analysts) can have already got been circulated before the official unhitch, inflicting prices to maneuver in anticipation. the price movement caused by the official news will thus be determined by but sensible the news is relative to the market's expectations, not but sensible it's in absolute terms.

In this chapter, I'll introduce variety of my ways in which, supported three elements:

(1) worth action,

(2) Technical indicators, and

Chart patterns. It's important to seek out out and observe all three parts at constant time. tho' some ways in which want exclusively technical indicators (such as Moving Average and VWAP), it's helpful to even have academic degree understanding of value action and chart patterns thus on become a created day bargainer. This understanding, particularly relating to value action, comes exclusively with observe.

As each day bargainer, you shouldn't care relating to corporations and their earnings. Day traders are not involved relating to what corporations do or what they produce. Your attention got to exclusively air value action, technical indicators and chart patterns. i do recognize loads of stock symbols than the names of actual corporations. i do not mingle basic analysis with technical analysis; I focus solely on the technical analysis. Now, having said that, as i mentioned in Chapters, I do probe for a basic catalyst, a reason why a stock is running up. If I even have a stock that is running up eightieth, i want to understand what the catalyst is, which i don't stop until I decide. "So, it is a biopharmaceutical stock which they merely got agency approval." or "They merely capable clinical trials. Okay, there is a catalyst, currently I will understand what's happening." on the so much aspect that, you won't understand ME listening in on conference calls or separation through the earnings papers. i do not care relating to those aspects as a results of i am not an extended term capitalist - i am each day bargainer. we've got an inclination to trade very quickly - guerrilla trading! – currently and so we have a tendency to exchange time periods as short as ten to thirty seconds. just in case you're skeptical ME on this point, i will be able to tell you from experience that in ten seconds you'll be able to produce thousands of dollars. I've done that. In ten seconds you will collectively lose thousands of bucks. I've done that too. Once the market moves quickly, you'd wish to make sure you are positioned inside the correct place to need advantage of the profits and cut back your risk exposure.

There square measure several traders out there and even millions loads of how. every bargainer needs their own strategy and edge. you'd wish to search out your spot inside the market where you're feeling snug. I concentrate on these ways in which as a results of these {are|ar|area unit|square MEasure} what work on behalf of me. I've come back to acknowledge in my mercantilism career that the best setups square measure the seven ways in which i will be able to be explaining throughout this chapter. These square measure easy ways in which in theory, but they are hard to master and wish several observe.

These mercantilism ways in which provide signals relatively occasionally and allow you to enter the markets throughout the quiet times, almost like the professionals do.

Another purpose to remember is that inside the market at once, over of the amount is recursive high frequency mercantilism. which means that you are mercantilism against computers. If you've ever contend chess against a portable computer, you acknowledge that you're eventually on the brink of lose. you would possibly get lucky once or double, but play spare times and you are certain to be the loser. a similar rule applies to recursive mercantilism. You're mercantilism stocks against portable computer systems. On the one hand, that represents a tangle. It means that the majority of changes in stocks simply} just square measure seeing square measure simply the results of computers moving shares around. On the other hand, it conjointly implies that there is a very little few stocks day when day that square measure on the brink of be mercantilism on such serious retail volume (as against institutional recursive trading) simply} just will overpower the recursive mercantilism and you which i, the retail traders, will management that stock. Each day, you wish to concentrate on mercantilism those specific stocks. These square measure what I call in Chapter four the Alpha Predators, stocks that square measure usually gapping up or down on earnings. you wish to go looking for the stocks that have vital retail traders' interest and vital retail volume. These square measure the stocks you will acquire, and along, we've got an inclination to the oldsters, the retail traders, will overpower the computers, almost like in associate extremely plot for succeeding killer sequel.

I head to head use the candlestick charts explained in Chapter half a dozen. each candlestick represents a amount of it slow. As i mentioned before, you will choose daily charts, hourly charts, 5-minute charts, even 1-minute charts. My preference is 5-minute charts as a results of i feel a 1-minute chart is simply too howling associated currently and so you will be misled by ancient value movement in an extremely 1-minute interval.

And please, remember, my philosophy of mercantilism is simply} just ought to master exclusively variety of solid setups to be consistently profitable. In fact, having an easy mercantilism methodology consisting of variety of lowest setups will work to cut back confusion and stress and allow you to concentrate loads of on the psychological side of mercantilism, that is what separates the winners from the losers.

ORDER ENTRY, EXIT AND TRADE MANAGEMENT

Before explaining my ways in which, it is vital to understand relating to my order entry, exit and trade management. Often, by the tip of the day, each square measure profitable, proving that have and trade management square measure loads of important than the stock and therefore the direction that traders select.

My trade size depends on the worth of the stock and on my account and risk management rule

1. I acquire 800 shares okay away.

2. I sell four hundred shares inside the initial target, transportation my stop loss to break-even (entry point).

3. 3. I sell another 200 shares inside following target purpose.

4. I generally keep the last 200 shares until i am stopped out. I invariably retain some shares just in case the prices keep occupancy my favor.

5. Some trained traders never enter the trade okay away. They scale into the trade, which means they patronise various points. they'll begin with 100 shares thus increase their position in

numerous steps. as an example, for a 1000-share trade, they enter either 500/500 or 100/200/700 shares. If done properly, usually|this can be} often an exquisite methodology of risk and trade management. However, managing the position throughout this technique is extremely hard. many new traders United Nations agency try to try to this may end up over-trading and may lose their benefit commissions, slippage and averaging down the losing trades.

I rarely scale into a trade but currently and so i am going to significantly in very very volume listed stocks. however bear in mind, scaling into a trade is also a ambiguous arm and beginners would possibly use it incorrectly as some way to average down their losing positions, feat sensible money once unhealthy. I don't advocate this system for beginners. tho' they'll appear similar, there is a massive distinction between scaling into a trade and averaging down a losing position. For beginners, averaging down a losing trade is also a instruction for wiping out your account, significantly with very little accounts that cannot stand several rounds of averaging down.

The ABCD Pattern is that the foremost easy and conjointly the most effective pattern to trade, and it is a terrific different for beginner and intermediate traders. tho' it's easy and has been acknowledged for a prolonged time, it still works very effectively as a results of many traders square measure still mercantilism it. As mentioned earlier, it's a self-fulfilling prophecy impact. you need to do in spite of all of the other traders do as a result of a trend is your friend. A trend would possibly alright be your exclusively friend.

Let's take a look at this pattern:

Example of academic degree ABCD Pattern.

ABCD Patterns begin with a strong upward move. customers square measure sharply buying a stock from purpose A and making constantly new highs of the day (point B). you would like to enter the trade, however you ought to not chase the trade, as a results of at purpose B it's very extended and already at a high value. in addition, you can not say where your stop got to be. you wish to never enter a trade while not knowing your stop.

At point B, traders bought the stock earlier begin slowly commerce it for profit and conjointly the prices come back down. Still you need to not enter the trade as a results of you don't apprehend where rock bottom of this pull back square measure. However, if you see that the worth does not come back down from a particular level, like purpose C, it means that the stock has found a attainable support. Therefore, you'll be able to set up your trade and created stops and a profit taking purpose.

Let's take a look at Ocean Power Technologies Iraqi National Congress. (ticker: OPTT) at Gregorian calendar month twenty 2, 2016, after they proclaimed that they'd a replacement $50 million contract to make a brand new ship. The stock surged up from $7.70 (A) to $9.40 (B) at around 9:40 a.m. I, beside many completely different traders United Nations agency had not detected the news, waited for purpose B thus a confirmation that the stock wasn't on the brink of go but a particular value (point C). when I saw that point C was holding as a support and customers wouldn't let the stock value go any but $8.10 (C), I bought 1,000 shares of OPTT on the point of C, and my stop was below purpose C. I knew that after the worth went higher, nearer to B, customers would climb on massively. As i mentioned before, the ABCD Pattern could be a very classic strategy and much of retail traders explore for it. I purchased stock between points B and C. {close to|on the brink of|near to|about to|getting prepared to|on the aim of} purpose D, the amount suddenly spiked, that meant that traders had jumped into the trade.

My exit would be once the stock created a replacement low, that was a sign of weakness. As you see, OPTT had a nice run up to around $12.

Let's contemplate another example, currently for SPU on August twenty 9, 2016. There are actually a pair of ABCD Patterns. I marked the second as abcd pattern. generally as a result of the mercantilism day progresses volumes become lower and therefore the second pattern is smaller in size. Please note simply} just can invariably have high volumes in points B and D (and in the end points b and d throughout this example).

Example of ABCD Pattern and abcd pattern.

To summarize my mercantilism strategy for the ABCD Pattern:

1. when I observe with my scanner or I'm prompt by someone in our chat area that a stock is stormy up from purpose A and reaching a large new high for the day (point B), I wait to look at if the worth makes a support on the far side purpose A. I call this point C. i do not jump into the trade quickly.

2. 2. I watch the stock throughout its consolidation quantity. i

choose my share size and stop and exit strategy.

3. 3. when I see that the worth is holding support at level C, I enter the trade on the brink of the worth of purpose C in anticipation of moving forward to purpose D or higher. 4. My stop is that the loss of purpose C. If the worth goes but purpose

4. C, I sell and accept the loss. Therefore, it is vital to buy for the stock {close to|on the brink of|near to|about to|getting prepared to|on the aim of} purpose C to cut back the loss. Some traders wait and acquire exclusively at purpose D to make sure that the ABCD Pattern is actual operative. In my opinion that is reducing your reward and increasing your risk.

5. If the worth moves higher, I sell [*fr1] my position at purpose D, and manufacture my stop higher to my entry purpose (break-even).

6. I sell the remaining position as shortly as my target hits or I feel that the worth is losing steam or that the sellers square measure deed management of the worth action.

In day mercantilism, Bull Flag is also a momentum fast execution strategy that generally works nice on low float stocks (Chapter 4). i feel Bull Flag is also a scalping strategy as a results of these flags won't last long and you wish to scalp the trade - get in quickly, take your profit, so get out.

Example of Bull Flag formation with one consolidation quantity.

This pattern is thought as Bull Flag as a results of it resembles a flag on a pole. In Bull Flag, you have got many huge candles rising (like a pole), and you moreover have a series of very little candles moving sideways (like a flag), or, as we've got an inclination to day traders say, "consolidating". Consolidation means that the traders that bought stocks at a less expensive value square measure presently commerce and taking their profits. though that's happening, the worth does not decrease sharply as a results of customers square measure still entering into trades and conjointly the sellers are not nonetheless up to the mark of the worth. many traders will miss obtaining the stock before the Bull Flag starts. it's risky to buy for stock once the worth is increasing. That's known as "chasing the stock". trained traders aim to enter the trade throughout quiet times and take their profits throughout wild times. That, of course, is that the overall opposite of but amateurs trade. They jump in or out once stocks begin to run, but grow bored and lose interest once the prices square measure, shall I say, sleepy.

Chasing the stocks is academic degree account killer for beginners. you wish to attend until the stock finds its part, thus anticipate the consolidation. As shortly as a result of the price breaks up inside the consolidation space, you will begin obtaining stocks.

Usually a Bull Flag will show several consolidation periods. I enter in just the first and second consolidation periods. Third associated higher consolidation periods square measure risky as a results of the worth has most likely been very extended in an extremely approach that indicates that the customers will shortly be losing their management. Let's study academic degree example of a Bull Flag of

RIGL on August thirty, 2016.

Example of Bull Flag formation with a pair of consolidation periods on RIGL.

This is academic degree example of two Bull Flag Patterns. it's normally hard to catch the first Bull Flag, and you may possibly miss it, but your scanner got to give you with a warning thereto. Let's contemplate academic degree example from my scanner throughout this point period:

Example of my intraday Bull Flag Strategy.

As you will see, my scanner showed RIGL at 12:36:15 pm. As shortly as I saw that, i detected that there was collectively a awfully high relative volume of mercantilism, that created this a perfect setup for day mercantilism. I waited for the first consolidation quantity to finish and, as shortly as a result of the stock began to maneuver towards its high for the day, I jumped into the trade. My stop loss would be the breakdown of the consolidation quantity. I marked my exit and entry inside the image below. As you'll be able to see, if you had required to attend for a second consolidation quantity in hope of the third Bull Flag, you'd possibly square measure stopped out. that is why I generally enter the first and second Bull Flags, but not the third one.

Entry, stop and exit of a Bull Flag Strategy on RIGL.

To summarize my mercantilism strategy:

when I see a stock stormy up (either on my scanner or once prompt by someone in our chatroom), I patiently wait until the consolidation quantity. i do not jump into the trade at once (you will recall that is the damaging act of "chasing").

1. I watch the stock throughout the consolidation quantity. i choose my share size and stop and exit strategy.

2. As shortly as prices square measure moving over the high of the consolidation candlesticks, I enter the trade. My stop loss is that the break below the consolidation periods.

3. I sell [*fr1] my position and take a profit on the so much. I bring my stop loss from the low of the consolidation to my entry value (break-even).

4. I sell my remaining positions as shortly as my target hits or I feel that the worth is losing steam and conjointly the sellers square measure acquiring of the worth action. As i mentioned, many of us, also as myself, acquire exclusively at or on the point of the escape (similar to the ABCD Pattern). The Bull Flag is largely academic degree ABCD Pattern which is able to happen loads of on low float stocks. It's fast and it will turn loads of quickly. Therefore, it is a heap of or less a Momentum Scalping Strategy. Scalpers acquire once a stock is running. They rarely want to get throughout consolidation (during that waiting and holding phase). These sorts of stocks generally drop quickly and brutally so it is vital for you to leap provided that there is a confirmation of jailbreak. anticipating the stocks to interrupt the best of a consolidation area is also a approach of reducing your risk and exposure time. instead of buying and holding and waiting, which will increase exposure time, scalpers merely anticipate the escape thus send their order. Get

in, scalp, and find out quickly. That's the philosophy of momentum scalpers:

- Get in at the escape
- Take your profit
- Get out of the approach

The Bull Flag Pattern is found inside associate uptrend in associate extremely stock.

BULL FLAG

The Bull Flag is also a long-based strategy. you need to not short a Bull Flag. I head to head don't trade loads of momentum. it's a risky strategy and beginners got to be very careful mercantilism these. If you opt on to, trade solely little size and exclusively once spare observe in simulators. you will collectively would love a super-fast execution system for scalping.

Top and Bottom Reversals square measure among the most effective mercantilism ways in which. Day traders love exploitation them as a result of they have a awfully made public entry and exit purpose and a really high profit-to-loss magnitude relation. during this section, I'm on the brink of create a case for the thanks to understand reversal setups exploitation scanners, the thanks to scan the Bollinger Bands to hunt out extremes, the thanks to use indecision or Doji candlesticks to need academic degree entry, the way to understand where to line your stops and your profit targets, and therefore the thanks to path your winners. If you are a a part of our private chat area, you will hear ME say time and time another time that what goes up, ought to come back down. Don't chase the trade if it's too extended. The inverse is in addition true. What goes down will definitely come back up to some extent. once a stock starts to unload considerably, there square measure a pair of reasons behind it:

1. Institutional traders and hedge funds have started commerce their huge position to the overall public market and conjointly the stock value is tanking.

2. Retail traders have started short selling the stock but they're going to got to cowl their shorts sooner or later. that is where you anticipate academic degree entry. Once short sellers try to cover their shorts, the stock will reverse. I'm on the brink of illustrate this strategy with variety of examples thus you will see exactly what to look for. Below is academic degree example of what it's want to appreciate a stock that's sold off terribly sect when the market opens. Moves like this square measure terribly hard to catch for the short facet, as a result of once you understand the stock, it's already too late to enter the short selling trade. But please, bear in mind the mantra: What goes up, ought to come back down. Therefore, you have the selection of expecting a reversal probability.

Example of a Reversal Strategy on point.

Each Reversal Strategy has four important elements:

1. A minimum of 5 candlesticks (5 min) moving upward or downward.
2. The stock is mercantilism on the brink of or outside of the Bollinger Bands. Bollinger Bands square measure academic degree indicator of volatility, and stocks generally keep inside these bands.

The stock will have academic degree extreme RSI indicator

(Relative Strength Index). academic degree RSI over ninety or below 10 will pique my interest. If you are not at home with what academic degree RSI indicator is, you'll be able to do a Google search or inquire from ME in our chat area. Your mercantilism platform will most likely have academic degree RSI indicator designed into it.

These three parts demonstrate that a stock is actual stretched, and you wish to pay shut attention to the scan for all of these info points. you wish to at a similar time explore for a particular RSI level, a particular vary of consecutive candles, and a particular position among the Bollinger Bands.

once the trend goes to end, generally indecision candles, sort of a whirligig or Doji, type that is once we have a tendency to got to be ready.

In reversal mercantilism, you are attempting to seek out one amongst these indecision candlesticks - spinning super or Dojis. they seem to be a sign that the trend would possibly shortly modification. A Doji is also a candle that encompasses a wick longer than its body. you will see a picture of a discouraged Doji below. it's that long higher wick that some would call a chief and tail that others would decision a plain radiation. This candle tells USA four things: the open value, the shut value, the high of that quantity and conjointly the low of that amount. So, once you have a candle with a chief tail, you acknowledge that at some purpose throughout that candle quantity the worth touched up, was unable to hold at that level, and was then sold off. It depicts barely of a battle taking place between the customers and conjointly the sellers inside that the patrons lost their push up. it's an honest indication that the sellers would possibly shortly management the worth and may push that value down. a similar is true a couple of optimistic Doji. you will collectively see a picture of a optimistic Doji below. it's that long lower wick that some would call a bottom tail et al. would decision a hammer. once you have a hammer candle with a bottom tail, you acknowledge that at some purpose throughout that candle amount the worth touched down, was unable to hold at those low levels, and was bought up. this means a battle between the customers and conjointly the sellers inside that the sellers lost their pull down. it's a wise indication that the customers would possibly presently gain management of the worth and push that value up.

Top Reversal Strategy with academic degree indecision visible light candlestick intentional as sign of entry. In reversal mercantilism, you explore for either Doji or indecision candlesticks. They're a symptom that the trend would possibly shortly modification. In Reversal ways in which, you are attempting to seek out a clear confirmation that the pattern is beginning to reverse. What you truly don't want is to air the wrong aspect of a reversal trade, or, as we've got an inclination to call it, "catching a falling knife". It doesn't sound kind of a wise plan in world associated it is not an honest set up in mercantilism. It means that once a stock is commerce off badly (the falling knife), you don't want to buy for on the concept that it got to bounce. If the stocks square measure dropping, you would like to attend for the confirmation of the reversal. this might generally be (1) the formation of a Doji or indecision candle and (2) the first 1-minute or the primary 5-minute candle to achieve a replacement high. that is my entry purpose. I set my stop at the lows. In reversal mercantilism, the RSI got to be at the extremes (above ninety, below 10), that final candle got to be outside the Bollinger Bands. Once you have your entry desires listed, you need to then explore for academic degree actual entry. academic degree entry on behalf of ME goes to be either the first 1-minute or the primary 5-minute candle to realize a replacement high.

When you've had a prolonged run of consecutive candles making new lows, the first candle that produces the new high is very vital. That's my entry purpose. There square measure times once I'll use the 1-minute chart, but usually I'll anticipate the 5-minute chart as a results of it is a means higher confirmation. The 5-minute chart is cleaner. the first 5-minute candle to make a replacement high is that the purpose at that i get inside the reversal, with a stop either at the low of the day or simply down around twenty to thirty cents. Usually, if a stock goes thirty cents against ME, I'll quit, acknowledge that I mistimed my entry, and investigate another time rather than still holds. At times, particularly on stocks that square measure dearer or loads of volatile, I'll simply use a 20- or 30-cent capricious stop if the low of the day is simply too remote.

Once you're in one amongst these trades, your exit indicators square measure quite easy. If the stock pops up and so suddenly moves turn back on a bottom bounce, you stop out for a loss. If you jump within the stock and it finally winds up merely going sideways, it's a sign simply} just square measure seemingly to look at a flag (a reverse flag), that could be a sign that the worth is probably on the brink of still drop. If i purchase in which i hold for variety of minutes and conjointly the price stays flat, I get out, notwithstanding what happens then i will be wrong, but so be it, I don't want to show my account to the unknown. i want to be inside the correct setup, and if it is not ready nonetheless, I'm out. If i commit the profit zone, i will be able to begin adjusting my stop, initial to break-even, thus to the low of the last 5-minute candle. i will be able to then keep adjusting my stop as I move up.

You must perceive that on the subject of all of the big moves will eventually be corrected. What goes up, should come back down. In Reversal ways in which, one amongst the foremost edges is that the possibility to seem at stocks that square measure running up, whereas at a similar time scheming possible resistance points associated areas that might provide an honest reversal probability. this permits you to resist being impulsive and dashing into the trade. you will instead take your time to seem at the trade develop and anticipate the momentum to begin to shift.

An important figure many traders use once talking relating to Reversal ways in which is that of a elastic. once stocks become terribly stretched to the downside, then inevitably they're due for a correction. So, once a stock is actual compression down, you will apprehend that at some purpose it's on the brink of produce a bounce, and you would like to be in there for the bounce. What you certainly don't want to be is to be the one still commerce. As I said before, that's like "catching a falling knife". If stocks square measure dropping, you would like to attend for the confirmation of the reversal. this may possibly be the first 1-minute or the primary 5-minute candle to make a replacement high.

That's my cue to leap in. I set my stop at the lows.

Bottom Reversal Strategy with academic degree indecision hammer candlestick intentional as sign of entry. This pretty illustration on in labor BioSolutions Iraqi National Congress. (EBS) shows a perfect reversal that I found exploitation my stock scanners. academic degree indecision candlestick at rock bottom of the downtrend signifies a attainable reversal, and as you see right later you see a large swing copy. I took this trade right once seeing indecision Doji, and unbroken my stop at the low of that indecision candle holder.

Example of a Reversal Strategy on EbS:

The biggest advantage of Reversal ways in which is that they overcome the difficulty of anticipating once stocks will produce major moves. you will possibly miss the moment once the stock starts to unload, and you won't have the time to short the stock for profit, but you will invariably indurate the reversal trade.

Another example:

Example of a Bottom Reversal Strategy on ALR.

I found ALR (Alere Iraqi National Congress.) on Gregorian calendar month twenty seven, 2016 at 10:57 a.m., using a software package program that scans the exchange and lets ME recognize exactly what i want to understand. See the image below:

Example of my Bottom Reversal real time scanner for ALR.

My scanner, at 10:57 a.m., showed ME that ALR had seven consecutive candles to the draw back, a relatively low float (80 million shares) and a relative volume of 1.21, that meant it had been mercantilism on the far side usual. i actually did not take this trade as a results of I incomprehensible my entry, however I required to point you what overall mercantilism ways in which seem as if for bottom reversals. once you're observant reversals, you would like to make sure simply} just exclusively trade extremes. the instance we've got an inclination to easily saw was a stock that created academic degree extreme move to the recoil before that move reversed. A stock that's been commerce off slowly all day long generally isn't applicable for a reversal.

Instead, it's helpful to place confidence in stocks the approach you're thinking that that of rubber bands - you would like to look at them extremely stretched to the recoil or, for temporary commerce, terribly stretched to the upside. you wish to look at the big extension, which means simply} just want to look at substantial volume. Once you are doing, you then explore for a couple of of key indicators which is able to counsel that the tide might even be preparing to show, and that's once you're taking the position. I've said it many times: what goes up, should come back down. typically these stocks will surrender days' and weeks' or years' worth of value gain in just a matter of minutes. it's very crucial to be able to time the reversal. I'll say it again: the key to the success with prime and bottom reversals is mercantilism the extremes.

How do I quantify these extremes? There square measure variety of things I look for: academic degree extreme RSI over ninety or below 10 will pique my interest

A candle outside of the Bollinger bands is in addition on the brink of interest ME.

Finally, seeing five to ten consecutive candles ending with academic degree indecision candle or a Doji is unquestionably on the brink of catch my interest. These candles generally show that sellers square measure losing their management whereas customers are becoming loads of powerful, that indicates the tip of a trend. I will add a caveat to that final point: there will be times once you may have five to ten consecutive candles whereas not loads of value action. they'll be drifting down slowly, however not quickly enough for you to sense that it's associate honest reversal. you wish to go looking for a mixture of those indicators all occurring at constant time. never sell short just because the prices square measure too high. you need to never argue with the crowd's decision, however it doesn't add up to you.

You do not got to run with the cluster - but you need to not run against it. Utilizing all of these numerous factors will manufacture the strategy that has been terribly created on behalf of me attributable to its impossible profit-to-loss magnitude relation. Your profit-to-loss magnitude relation is your average winners versus your average losers. many new traders end up mercantilism with a awfully poor profit-to-loss quantitative relation as a results of they sell their winners timely which they hold their losers too long. this can be an especially common habit among new traders. The Reversal Strategy, however, lends itself to having a much bigger profit-to-loss magnitude relation. to return to the rubber band analogy, by following such a method you will invariably acquire stocks once the rubber band is stretched as means as a result of it'll go. once you time this right, you're in as a result of the rubber band snaps back and you will then ride the momentum right copy.

To summarize my mercantilism strategy for rock bottom Reversal Strategy:

I created a scanner that show ME stocks with four or loads of consecutive candlesticks going downward. when I see a stock hit my scanner, I quickly review the amount associated level of resistance or support on the point of the stock to look at if it's an honest trade or not.

I anticipate confirmation of a Reversal Strategy: (1) formation of a discouraged Doji or indecision candle, (2) candlesticks being very shut or outside of the Bollinger Bands, and (3) the RSI ought to be but 10.

when I see the stock produce a replacement 5-minute high, I acquire the stock.

My stop loss is that the low of the previous red candlestick or the low of the day.
My profit target is (1) succeeding level of support or (2) VWAP (Volume

Weighted Average

Price, delineate later throughout this chapter) or moving averages or (3) the stock makes a replacement 5- minute high, which means that the customers square measure another time capture.

A prime Reversal is similar to a Bottom Reversal, but on a short commerce facet. Let's take a look at Bed bathing tub & on the so much aspect Iraqi National Congress. as a result of it listed on June 23, 2016. My scanner showed BBBY rising at 10:18 a.m. with six consecutive candles. It had a relative volume of twenty one fifty that meant it had been mercantilism significantly on the far side usual. That was as a results of, as mentioned, retail traders explore for uncommon mercantilism volume.

I took this trade associated created an honest profit on it. The candlesticks weren't outside of the Bollinger Bands, but as a results of it had been mercantilism with very uncommon volume, and forming a nice Doji on prime, i made a decision to need the trade. I shorted stock once a replacement 5-minute candlestick was created, with my stop being the break of the high of the last 5-minute candles. I coated my shorts at $43.40 for a 60cent profit once the stock created a replacement 5-minute high.

Example of my prime Reversal real time scanner for BBBY.

Example of a chief Reversal Strategy on BBBY.

To summarize my mercantilism strategy for the best Reversal Strategy:

I created a scanner that confirmed stocks with four or loads of consecutive candlesticks moving upward. when I see the stock hit my scanner, I quickly review the amount associated level of resistance or support on the point of the stock to look at if it's an honest trade or not.

I anticipate confirmation of a Reversal Strategy: (1) formation of a discouraged Doji or indecision candle, (2) candlesticks being very shut or outside of Bollinger Bands, and (3) the RSI ought to be on the far side ninety.

when I see the stock produce a replacement 5-minute low, I begin short selling the stock.

My stop square measure the high of the previous candlestick or simply the high of the day.

My profit target is (1) succeeding level of support or (2) VWAP or moving averages or (3) once the stock makes a replacement 5-minute high, which means the customers square measure another time seizure. Some day traders focus exclusively on reversal trades and really base their entire careers on them. Reversal trades square measure undoubtedly the foremost classic of the numerous ways in which with a awfully high risk-reward magnitude relation and, apparently, you will invariably understand stocks that square measure sensible candidates for reversal trades. i really am mercantilism loads of and additional reversal trades latterly, significantly throughout late morning and afternoon mercantilism. However, reversal mercantilism is not nonetheless the cornerstone of my mercantilism ways in which. i am loads of of a VWAP bargainer and Support or Resistance merchant.

Some traders use moving averages as potential entry and exit points for day mercantilism. several stocks will begin academic degree upside or recoil trend respecting their moving averages in 1-minute and 5-minute charts as reasonably a moving support or resistance line. Traders can have the advantage of this behavior and ride the trend on moving average (on prime of moving average for going long or below moving average for temporary selling).

I have been asked why moving averages are becoming support or resistance, and conjointly the solution is as a result of many traders square measure observant these lines and making choices supported them. Therefore, they need a self-fulfilling prophecy impact. there isn't any basic reason behind moving averages being a support or resistance line.

I use 9 and twenty exponential moving averages (EMA) and fifty and 200 easy moving averages (SMA). I won't are available the most points of what moving averages square measure and conjointly the variations between easy and exponential thus on keep this book short. You can, however, do a Google search and understand information relating to these moving averages otherwise you may in the end contact ME directly through network.Vancouver-Traders.com with any queries you'll need. Your charting software package can haves most of the moving averages intrinsic . they are able to be used and there is no would love to vary the default setting in them.

Let's take a look at the chart below for NUGT to look at but you will trade supported 9 EMA in associate extremely 1-minute chart.

Example of a Moving Average Trend Strategy on NUGT.

As you will see, at 15:06 pm I detected NUGT has intentional a Bull Flag. I saw that a consolidation amount was happening on prime of 9 EMA. As shortly as I saw that 9 EMA was holding as a result of the support, I jumped on the trade and rode the trend until the worth bust the moving average at 15:21 pm. I've marked my entry and exit points on the chart. Let's take a look at another example, Celgene

Corporation (CELG), on June 16, 2016. within the chart below, you will see but you will trade supported twenty EMA in associate extremely 1-minute chart. I marked my entry and exit points on the chart.

To summarize my mercantilism strategy for Moving Average Trend Trading:

when i'm observation a stock and spot a trend is respecting moving average, I contemplate trend mercantilism. I quickly contemplate the previous days' mercantilism info to look at if the stock is responding to those moving averages in associate extremely 1-minute or 5-minute chart. I even have 9 and twenty EMA and fifty and 200 SMA.

Once I learn that moving average could be a heap of applicable to the behavior of the trade, I get the stock once confirmation of moving averages as a support, which i acquire as shut as possible to the moving average line (in order to possess a bit stop). My stop will generally be 5 cents below the break of moving average line.

I ride the trend until the break of moving average. I never use trailing stops which i constantly monitor the trend with my eyes.

If the stock is moving terribly high faraway from the moving average, I take some profit, typically at half-position. i do not invariably wait until the break of moving average for my exit.

I head to head don't trade fairly typically supported moving averages. I contemplate them to look at potential levels of support or resistance, but I rarely produce any trend trade based totally upon their trend as a results of, in an exceedingly trend trade strategy, and you're generally exposed inside the marketplace for a considerable time. Some trend trades can last as long as several hours that is simply too long for my temperament. Another major draw back I even have with Moving Average Trending is simply} just don't apprehend inside the stock you would like to trade that moving average is accurately engaging at a support or resistance level. inside the examples over, if I changed my moving average from 9 to 12, or to 15, or to the other vary, then it won't act as a nice clean support.

I use 9 and twenty EMA on my default charts, but i do recognize no person can. Some traders square measure exploitation eleven and twenty one EMA. That inside the end is also a vital draw back with Moving Average mercantilism. You don't apprehend that moving average is best for a stock and you clearly haven't got enough time to ascertain all of them out throughout the mercantilism day.

I recommend exploitation either: nine, twenty EMA and fifty and 200 SMA or: 11, twenty one EMA and fifty and 200 SMA

Having said that, Moving Average Trend Strategy could be a terrific strategy for beginners, as a result of it always does not want a awfully fast method} method and trade execution. in addition, stop loss and entry points is clearly recognized from the moving average on the charts.

As i discussed, ways in which have faith in your account size, temperament, science of mercantilism and risk tolerance, likewise as on your software package and conjointly the tools and brokers simply} just have. the mix of all of these factors have diode ME to be a VWAP bargainer and support or resistance merchant, one factor i am going to create a case for inside following section. However, i want to stress that trade methods are not one factor that you simply can imitate simply from reading a book, speaking with a mentor, or attending a class. you have to slowly and methodologically develop your preferred method thus continue it. there is nothing wrong with any strategy if it works for you.

There is no sensible and unhealthy in any of these strategies; it really is also a matter of personal different. currently let ME create a case for what my favorite mercantilism ways in which square measure.

Volume Weighted Average value, or VWAP, is that the foremost vital technical indicator in day mercantilism. Definitions of VWAP is found in every Wikipedia and much of various on-line resources. i will be able to skip explaining it well for the sake of keeping this guide short, but primarily, VWAP could be a moving average that takes into account the volumes of the stock being listed. completely different moving averages square measure calculated based totally exclusively on the worth of the stock inside the chart, but VWAP collectively considers the amount of the shares that the stock is listed on every value. Your mercantilism platform most likely has VWAP designed into it and you will use it whereas not dynamical its default setting. VWAP is also a wise indicator of United Nations agency is up to the mark of the worth action - customers or sellers. once stock is listed over VWAP, it means that the customers square measure in overall management of the worth. once a stock value breaks below the VWAP, it's safe to assume that the sellers square measure capture over the worth action.

Trading supported VWAP is extremely easy for beginner traders as a results of such an oversized quantity of traders square measure learning the VWAP and making choices supported it. Therefore, a beginner bargainer can merely get on the right facet of the trade. once a stock tries to interrupt the VWAP but cannot, {you'll|you can|you may} short stock as a results of you will safely assume that completely different traders that square measure observance will begin to short.

A mercantilism strategy supported VWAP is also an easy and easy strategy to follow. I generally short stocks once traders attempt but fail to interrupt the VWAP in 5-minute charts. Let's take a look at a recent trade that I took on SolarCity Corporation (SCTY) on St John's Day, 2016. At around 10:30 a.m. on June 24, 2016, I detected that SCTY had found a support over VWAP. I purchased one,000 shares of the stock with the anticipation of moving toward $22 with VWAP as a support. My stop was an in depth below VWAP. I initial sold alittle position at $22.50, and so rapt my stop to break-even. I sold another position at $22 as a results of i do recognize half-dollars (such as $1.50, $2.50, $3.50) and whole dollars ($1, $2, $3) generally act at a support or resistance level.

VWAP collectively works well once you would like to short stocks. Let's take a look at another recent trade that I took on SolarCity Corporation, currently on Gregorian calendar month twenty 2, 2016, and currently on the short facet.

Example of a short VWAP Strategy on SCTY.

At around eleven a.m., I detected that SCTY had featured a resistance over VWAP. I shorted the stock with the anticipation of losing the

VWAP at around $23. Around twelve pm customers gave up and conjointly the sellers took management of the worth action. I had a nice run all the means all the way down to $22 associated coated my shorts at $22 for an honest $1,000 profit.

To summarize my mercantilism strategy for VWAP trading:

when I produce my watch list for the day, I monitor the worth action around VWAP. If a stock shows respect toward VWAP, then I wait until a confirmation of the VWAP break or support.

I generally acquire as shut as possible to cut back my risk. My stop square measure a chance and shut 5-minute chart below VWAP.

I keep the trade until I hit my profit target or till I reach a replacement support or resistance level.

4. I generally sell half-positions on the point of the profit target or support or resistance level and move my on the point of my entry purpose or break-even.

A similar approach will work equally likewise once you short a stock.

Horizontal support or resistance mercantilism is my favorite kind of mercantilism. The market doesn't recognize diagonals. It remembers value levels, that square measure why horizontal support or resistance lines add up, but diagonal trend lines square measure subjective and receptive self-deception. I thus avoid trend lines as a results of, in my opinion, they are wildly subjective and cause fancy and self-deceit. In fact, trend lines square measure among the foremost deceptive of all tools. You'll draw a line across the prices or zones in associate extremely approach which is able to modification its slope and its message. If you're in an exceedingly mood to buy for, as an example, you will draw your line somehow vessel.

After making thousands of trades and looking out at thousands of charts, I've come back to the conclusion that the market doesn't apprehend diagonals. It remembers value levels, that square measure why horizontal support or resistance lines add up, but diagonal trend lines square measure subjective and receptive selfdeceit. Support is also a indicant where buying is powerful enough to interrupt or reverse a downtrend.

When a downtrend hits support, it bounces kind of a diver hits rock bottom of the ocean and so automatically pushes faraway from it. Support is delineate on a chart by a horizontal line connecting a pair of or loads of bottoms (see the figure below). Resistance is also a indicant where commerce is powerful enough to interrupt or reverse academic degree uptrend. once academic degree uptrend hits resistance, it acts kind of a 1 that hits their head on a branch whereas rise a tree - they stop and should even tumble down. Resistance is delineate on a chart by a horizontal line connecting a pair of or loads of super.

Minor support or resistance causes trends to pause, whereas major support or resistance causes them to reverse. Traders patronise support and sell at resistance, making their effectiveness a self-fulfilling prophecy. exploitation this system, every morning I order the stocks that i'd want to trade supported the standards I set forth in previous Chapter: a stock that has basic catalysts like news, associate extreme operating statement or a replacement drug approval. These stocks square measure those who retail traders square measure observation and getting to trade.

Before the market opens, I'm going back to the daily charts and understand value levels that square measure shown inside the past to be crucial. Finding grant or resistance levels is tough and wishes mercantilism experience. If you watch ME mercantilism every morning, you will see but I place my support or resistance lines on my Alpha Predators.

Support or resistance lines in daily charts are not invariably easy to hunt out, and currently and so you will not be able to draw one thing clear. If I cannot see one thing clear, I don't got to draw one thing. there's associate honest chance that completely different traders won't see these lines clearly and therefore there's no purpose in forcing myself to draw support or resistance lines. during this case, i am going to organize my trades supported the VWAP or Moving Averages or chart patterns that I earlier mentioned.

Here square measure some hints for drawing support or resistance lines:

you will generally see indecision candles (Chapter 6) inside the area of support or resistance as a result of that is where customers and sellers square measure closely fighting each other.

Half-dollars and whole dollars generally act at a support or resistance level. If you don't understand a support or resistance line around these numbers on daily charts, detain mind that in intraday these numbers can act as associate invisible support or resistance line.

you need to invariably contemplate the recent info to draw lines.

The loads of a line that is touching value lines, the {a heap|tons|plenty|heaps|loads|a great deal} of that the road is also the next support or resistance and incorporates a lot of value. provide that line loads of stress.

exclusively the support or resistance lines inside the present value vary square measure important. If the worth of the stock is presently $20, there isn't any purpose to seek out support or resistance lines inside the region once it had been $40. it's unlikely that the stock will move and reach that area. notice solely the support or resistance area that is on the brink of your day mercantilism vary.

Support or resistance lines are actually academic degree "area" and not precise numbers. as an example, once you understand a district around $19.69 as a support line, you wish to expect value action movement around that vary but not at exactly $19.69. reckoning on the worth of the stock, a district of 5 to 10 cents is safe to assume. inside the instance with a support line of $19.69, the $64000 support area would be one thing from $19.62 to $19.72.

the worth ought to have a clear bounce from that level. If you are not sure if the worth has bounced during this level, then it's possibly not a support or resistance level.

For day mercantilism, it's higher to draw support or resistance lines across the extraordinary prices instead of across areas where the bulk of the bars stopped. usually|this can be} often the entire opposite of swing mercantilism. For swing mercantilism, you'd wish to draw support or resistance lines across the perimeters of congestion areas where the bulk of the bars stopped rather than across the intense prices. inserting support or resistance lines, tho' robust, is absolutely quite easy once you get the droop of it.

Let's review a recent trade that I took supported these lines. CarMax (ticker: KMX), the United States' largest used-car distributer, on June 21, 2016 had extreme earnings and its stock gapped down over thirddimensional. That was a perfect probability for retail traders like ME to hunt out associate honest trade set up. I quickly found the support or resistance area level on a daily chart and watched the worth action around those levels. My watch list Gapper on midsummer, 2016 at 9:20 a.m. KMX is academic degree Alpha Predator for that day. KMX support or resistance lines and my trade for that day. when reviewing the daily charts, I found a pair of levels of $48.09 and $48.48. Once the market opened, I watched the stock and accomplished that the globe of around forty eight.09 acted as a support. When

I saw academic degree indecision candle around the support line, I purchased one thousand shares of KMX with a stop of below $48. The stock surged up toward succeeding level at $48.48 and, apparently enough, $48.48 was collectively on the brink of my invisible half-round vary ($48.50). I sold [*fr1] my position for a profit and unbroken the balance for going higher. Since I did not have the opposite support or resistance area higher than, i created a choice to sell my remaining position at the invisible resistance line of $49. As you will see, $49 acted as a strong resistance line, and conjointly the stock sold faraway from that level.

To summarize my mercantilism strategy for support or resistance trading: each morning, when I produce my watch list for the day, I quickly contemplate the daily charts for my watch list and understand the globe of support or resistance.

I monitor the worth action around those areas on a 5-minute chart. If academic degree indecision candle forms around that area, that is the confirmation of the quantity which i enter the trade. I typically get as shut as possible to cut back my risk. Stop would be a chance and an in depth 5-minute chart below support or resistance level.

I'll take profit on the point of succeeding support or resistance level.

I keep the trade open until I hit my profit target or I reach a replacement support or resistance level.

I generally sell half-positions on the point of the profit target or support or resistance level and move my on the point of my entry purpose for break-even.

If there are no next obvious support or resistance levels, i am going to place confidence in closing my trade at or on the point of half-dollar or round-dollar levels. an identical approach can work once you short a stock.

You have presently scan in brief relating to my mercantilism strategy. You'll be inquisitive what completely different traders do. As i mentioned before, there square measure unlimited numbers of mercantilism ways in which folks have developed for themselves. Traders generally choose their ways in which supported such factors as account size, amount of it slow which is able to be dedicated to mercantilism, mercantilism experience, temperament and risk tolerance. you ought to develop your own strategy. A mercantilism strategy is very personalized to each individual. My risk tolerance and science square measure probably utterly completely different from yours and from those of various traders. I'd not be cozy with a $500 loss, but someone encompasses a vast account can merely hold onto the loss and eventually produce profit out of a losing trade. you can not mirror-trade anyone else; you wish to develop your own risk management methodology and strategy.

Some traders focus heavily on technical indicators a bit like the RSI, the moving average convergence divergence (also observed because the MACD), or the moving average crossover. There square measure a full bunch, if not thousands, of refined technical indicators out there. Some traders believe they have found the Holy Grail of technical indicators, and it might be a mixture of RSI or the moving average crossover. i do not believe any of them. I don't assume that they work for day mercantilism, significantly over the long run. a number of my day bargainer colleagues would possibly bother ME, but my personal experience is that you simply cannot enter a trade with a general approach thus let indicators dictate your entry and exit. that is my next rule:

Rule 10: Indicators exclusively indicate; they have to not be allowed to dictate.

Computers square measure mercantilism all of the time. once you created a system for mercantilism that has no input or needs no choices by the bargainer, then you are coming back into the world of recursive mercantilism, and you may lose trades to investment banks that have million-dollar algorithms and billions of bucks in cash for mercantilism. Of course, i benefit of the RSI in my scanner for a couple of of my mercantilism ways in which, and significantly for reversal mercantilism. Obviously, I even have scanners that place confidence in an exceedingly high or low RSI, but those square measure loads of conditioned to hunt out stocks at extremes. usually|this can be} often not by any suggests that a acquire or sell indicator.

You must still understand your own place inside the market. i will be a 1-minute or a 5-minute trader; you will be a 60-minute bargainer. Some might even be daily or weekly traders (swing traders). There's an area inside the marketplace for everyone. place confidence in what you are learning throughout this book as things of a puzzle that on compose the larger image of mercantilism. you are on the brink of acquire some things here, you're on the brink of devour things on your own from your own reading and analysis, and, overall, you will manufacture a puzzle which is able to rework your own distinctive mercantilism strategy. i do not expect everything I do to work exactly a similar for you. i am happy to help you develop a method that is on the brink of work for you, your temperament, your account size and your risk tolerance.

The key for now's simply} just master one strategy. Once you will tread water inside the market together with your one strategy, you will be a bargainer whereas not reproof your account. usually|this can be} often simply a matter of paying time inside the chair. The longer you pay observance your charts, the loads of you will learn. usually|this can be} often employment where you survive until you will produce it. You'll begin casting out later, however initial you'd wish to master only 1 strategy. it's the VWAP trade, it's a Bull Flag Momentum Strategy, it's a Reversal Strategy, otherwise you may manufacture a way of your own. slender the alternatives down, develop that area of strength into a practicable strategy, thus use that strategy to survive until you are able to develop others.

It is totally crucial for every bargainer to be mercantilism a way. organize a trade, and trade the organize. I want someone had said to ME when I initial started work, "Andrew, you'd wish to trade a method. If you are mercantilism with real money, you wish to be mercantilism a written strategy, and it ought to have historical info to verify that it's worth mercantilism with real money." you can not modification your set up once you have got already entered the trade associate degreed have associate open position.

The truth relating to traders is that they fail. They lose money, associated an outsized proportion of those traders aren't getting the education simply} just square measure receiving from this book. they are on the brink of be exploitation live mercantilism ways in which are not even beat out, they're going to merely be haphazardly mercantilism a bit of this and barely of that until their account is gone, thus they're going to marvel what happened. You don't want to live trade a replacement strategy until you've proved that it's worth finance in. you will observe three months on a machine, thus trade very little size with real cash for one month, thus come back to the machine to work on your mistakes or observe new ways in which for a new three months. There's no shame in going back to a machine at any stage of your day mercantilism career. Even seasoned and trained traders, once they need to develop a replacement strategy, check it out on a live machine initial.

Your focus whereas reading this book and active in simulated accounts got to be to develop a method worth mercantilism, and it's my pleasure to assist you thereupon methodology. Remember, the market is commonly on the brink of be there. you do not got to rush this. each day mercantilism career is also a marathon and not a sprint. it is not relating to making $50,000 by the tip of next week. It's concerning developing a set of skills which is able to last a life.

Day mercantilism involves buying and mercantilism constant security among a similar day with a scan to making a quick exploit changes inside the price. These intraday traders produce money by skimming very little profits on high mercantilism volumes. They amplify these profits by borrowing on margin. A businessperson buys 10 CFDs on Apple stock within the morning expecting a positive quarterly earnings announcement within the afternoon, thus places academic degree order to sell the stock once the price rises $5. The Apple stock value is $175 (x 10 shares = $1,750], but the businessperson is solely required to pay a twenty 5 p.c margin rate (or $43.75 x 10 shares = $437.50). once Apple announces record-blowing iPhone sales, the stock rises to $180 and so the limit order is dead for a profit of $50.

A speculator shorts academic degree e-mini unit of measurement by-product once the short moving average crosses below the long moving average, with a 2 pip stop-loss. The margin rate is twenty 5 p.c of the $1,100 contract.

Trading volume spikes and one minute later the trade executes once the price falls 2 pips.

ALGORITHMIC TRADERS

Algorithmic traders execute in fractions of a second. They develop programs to identify discrepancies in prices across thousands of securities. These clever bots acquire and sell securities in milliseconds.

Before you start day mercantilism, confirm you're at home with the next margin rules and account limits.

- Day mercantilism – Day mercantilism involves finishing a visit trade on constant day. If a businessperson buys a security thus sells it on constant day, it's thought of daily trade. Conversely, if a businessperson sells short a security and buys it on constant day, it's thought of daily trade.

- Margin mercantilism – Most day traders borrow money from brokers to trade. mercantilism on margin involves victimization the money associated securities in an extremely broker account as collateral for the loan. what proportion the businessperson can borrow to trade is based on his risk profile and so the worth of the investment account (cash + securities). The magnitude relation of the quantity inside the account to the quantity borrowed is called leverage.

- Pattern mercantilism – inside the America markets, day traders square measure thought of pattern traders if they borrow on margin, trade constant security four or loads of times among five business days, and day mercantilism is six p.c of the trade activity for that quantity. Once daily businessperson is taken under consideration a pattern merchant, they are required to require care of a minimum balance of $25,000 to day trade. This balance is additionally a mixture of cash and securities. The pattern day mercantilism rule does not apply to futures mercantilism, making futures a popular day mercantilism instrument.

- Call – If the price of the investment account falls below the maintenance margin, the businessperson will have several days to revive the account maintenance balance through cash and/or securities.

- Leverage – Leverage is that the buying power gained through margin disposal expressed as a magnitude relation of the quantity inside the account to the quantity borrowed. If you have the $25,000 pattern mercantilism minimum in your account and square measure allowed 4:1 leverage, you will be able to borrow up to $100,000 to trade.

Popular mercantilism ways in which have associate large influence on value movement. once traders trade constant pattern, they contribute to the sustaining of the pattern. {the worth|the value|the value} intelligence inside the simple candlestick provides key price movement indications for many traders. If this were all there was to mercantilism, we'd all be created. many others factors can influence value, along side economic news, company earnings reports, and political events. the foremost vital trades that have the foremost influence on value square measure generally hidden on dark pools, which allow large traders to trade whereas not exposing their value or volume levels. usually|this can be} often so you cannot trade supported the data that, as an example, associate large hedge fund is on the purpose of sell all its shares in Facebook. If this information were to be created public, all traders would rush to sell their Facebook stock before the inevitable value decline.

Trend mercantilism – The trend is your friend, if you will be able to follow it. In academic degree uptrend, trend traders draw diagonal lines upwards that trace higher highs and higher lows. in associate extremely downtrend, the downward-sloping lines follow lower lows and lower highs. mercantilism volume is also a wise indicator of whether or not or not or not the trend will continue.

Breakouts – The escape businessperson uses historical rating info to forecast future value movements. value resistance levels square measure established once the price has reached constant high multiple times (often 3x). Support levels sort where the price hits constant lows. The businessperson will set academic degree entry purpose once the price breaks through a resistance or injury.

Momentum – The momentum behind a value movement square measure typically academic degree indicator of what proportion strength is behind a value trend. If mercantilism volume is powerful, the trend could be a heap of attainable to be sustained whereas weak mercantilism volume might signal a value reversal.

Pivot Points – These well-liked value trend indicators take a mercantilism session's highs, lows and shut to predict the price trend inside following mercantilism quantity. The mercantilism quantity square measure typically on the order of minutes or months.

Scalping – Scalpers produce money by taking very little profits across many trades. They exit as soon as a trade starts losing money rather than wait around hoping the price will reverse. the limited gains can add up to associate large profit.

Retracement – prices seldom initiate on academic degree upward physical phenomenon whereas not retracing their movements down. Retracers decide to predict that retracement signals associate large value reversal. They increase their profit potential by buying inside the retracement before prices reverse. Fibonacci ratios square measure well-liked retracement levels (23.6%, 38.2%, 61.8%).

No strategy is consistently reliable but they're going to provide a symptom of once a value trend goes to continue or reverse. Most day traders combine quite one mercantilism strategy and indicator.

People generally raise whether or not or not stock mercantilism is passive gain. However, the answer will rely upon your individual approach. Active traders will invest a considerable amount of it slow and energy into turning a profit. In fact, their trade activity will generally be their primary focus.

Whereas, if you're desirous to get a passive gain from day mercantilism, you nearly actually don't pays all day at your portable computer observation the markets and making trades. not like active traders, your passive gain will match around your means, rather than dictate it. So, if you would like to induce passive gain from selections or bitcoin mercantilism, as an example, you may want at render your capital to a trustworthy broker, automated system or invest via copy mercantilism.

Before we have a tendency to look at some techniques and tips to earning passive gain day mercantilism, it's necessary you understand every the benefits and downsides. The restricted amount of it slow you will got to commit could be a accessible profit. However, this in addition implies that there is increased pressure on the investment selections you're doing produce.

In addition, passive mercantilism can usually cause a slower stream of profit once place next to active mercantilism. there is in addition a danger {that you|that you merely|that you just} simply will neglect observation your passive gain. this may cause losing out on potential profits. As another, you may pay such loads time worrying relating to your positions {that you|that you merely|that you just} simply to a fault interfere, limiting returns.

To make day mercantilism passive gain easy, some intercommunicate automation. Used properly, automated systems would possibly modification you to induce substantial profits. usually|this can be} often as a results of there is exclusively a definite style of trades you will be able to manually produce each day. Whereas a cultured formula can automatically enter and exit positions as soon as pre-determined criteria square measure met.They in addition modification you to trade style of markets promptly. In fact, once you have programmed in your criteria, you will be able to generate passive gain whereas you are sleeping.

Some would possibly clearly doubt the effectively of these systems. However, concerning seventy fifth of all trades created on the massive apple stock exchange and so the data system presently originate from these algorithms, demonstrating their capabilities.

Before you will be able to begin developing a passive gain through automated stocks mercantilism, as an example, you will got to notice the right coding system. Do your analysis and check reviews before you invest in any. In fact, for steering and examples, see our coding system page. Once you have chosen a coding system, you will got to develop associate economical strategy. creating a listing of your day mercantilism parameters is sometimes associate honest place to start. you may want to ponder the following:

- When to enter and exit positions
- Position size
- Intraday mercantilism timeframe
- Targets and stop-losses
- Algorithm

Once you have developed a way, you will got to have the formula written. If you have some technical info you may be able to input directions yourself, as a result of the code is relatively easy. However, if not, you may want to ponder hiring a mortal to assist you.

Before you will be able to use associate automatic system to induce a passive gain with bitcoin, as an example, you in addition got to backtest your strategy. this permits you're taking a glance at your system before you risk any capital. you only run your coding system against historical value info to urge a gauge for the means well it performs. you will be able to then establish and remedy any issues.

The Monte Carlo simulation is also a helpful gizmo to undertake. This repeatedly tests steps of your formula and inputs random info into your parameters. this might alter you to forecast but well your new system goes to perform.

With the labor hopefully done, you will be able to presently get pleasure from wanting that passive gain build up in your account. However, you will got to routinely check your coding system is performing arts clearly. Technical glitches and anomalies can occur.

Arguably, otherwise for mercantilism passive gain to be created easy is through copy mercantilism. rather than devoting goodish time and energy into developing a way and observation the markets, you will be able to just like the success of veteran traders. you merely choose a businessperson thus a programme will mimic that trader's buying and mercantilism along side your capital. However, generally {you may|you'll|you can} notice the traders and so the net website will take a bit proportion of your profit. In fact, those who imitate traders may additionally then be derived and earn commissions.

You may be thinking usually|this can be} often the proper because of begin forex mercantilism as passive gain. However, whether or not or not it's stocks, futures or forex, there keep sure drawbacks to consider:

Risking capital – you wish to be prepared that because of the volatility of markets, you will lose all the capital you at the beginning endowed. If you're considerably risk-averse, seeing large losses for a couple of of days would possibly even stop you sleeping.

Choosing a businessperson – selecting a merchant is no simple challenge. as an example, academic degree aggressive crypto businessperson would possibly clear you are available several days. So, ponder their instrument of choice and approach. Also, check their recent trade history. you would like steady and consistent results. it's value noting, however, some folks really notice several veteran traders to repeat.

Not Following Trades proportionately – Some sites won't alter you to trade proportionately. However, for good, if not clear reasons, traders generally invest specific quantities. So, make sure you truly follow repetition your businessperson.

Learning tool vs secure money generator – many argue trade repetition is best used as a tool by beginners to be told relating to utterly completely different markets and instruments. So, bear in mind it shouldn't be the best suggests that to induce a passive gain day mercantilism.

Overall, for those fascinated by day mercantilism for passive gain, you may want to ponder every methods on prime of. each might significantly cut back the quantity of it slow you have to pay intraday mercantilism. However, it's in addition value highlight they're out there with drawbacks and risks. Therefore, the challenge is deciding which may suit your individual needs and means.

Before you choose day mercantilism is that the correct manner for you to induce a passive gain, there square measure sure rules and rules value considering. Some tax systems split earning kinds into three distinct categories:

Passive – generally thought of net financial gain and financial gain from a business inside that the payer does not materially participate. it's going to conjointly embrace self-charged interest. This definition encompasses a broad vary of activities. To comprise this bracket you wish to not be too involved in your intraday trade activities.

Portfolio – Capital gains from securities and commodities mercantilism, like stocks, currencies, gold, ETFs, etc, is commonly thought of portfolio gain. However, it ought to or won't even be thought of passive gain.

Active – as a result of the name suggests, you wish to be endlessly and well committed the endeavor. If you were to pay most of your day engaged in intraday mercantilism, as an example, you'd comprise this category.

These definitions vary to some extent as you progress between utterly completely different tax jurisdictions. The point, however, is that it's wise check what reasonably trade activity will represent passive gain where you reside, and whether or not or not there any express tax rules you'd wish to bear in mind of.

Many countries ponder passive gain assessable like nonpassive financial gain. However, it's going to even be treated otherwise. as an example, in the US, the bureau permits passive losses to be written off exclusively against passive gains. So, once losses exceed the gain from passive day mercantilism activities, the rest of the loss square measure typically carried forward to succeeding tax year, as long as there is some passive gain to put in writing down it off against.

For extremely booming traders, some advisors will counsel structures that embrace multiple entities to maximise the tax and protection edges.

although the actual structure is set by academic degree individual's financial goals, it perpetually includes a C corporation, that exists to be the ultimate partner or managing member of the many liability companies. throughout this way, extra gain square measure typically transferred to the corporate entity (usually up to 30 minutes of revenue) through a shrunken management fee to need advantage of the additional tax ways in which on the market.

For example, to fund faculty expenses or to gift kids money tax-free , relations can become workers. The corporation can then create the foremost of deductible salaries and education expenses, whereas building Social Security and health care accounts. Medical compensation plans square measure typically created to fund all types of elective health care and medical premium. Retirement accounts like IRAs and 401(k)s square measure typically transferred into a 401a, academic degree ERISA pension fund that allows contributions of up to $49,000 annually and should never be attacked by creditors or through a legal claim. as a results of the corporation pays taxes on lucre, the goal is to pay as many expenses as possible with pretax greenbacks and to attenuate assessable gain.

This type of business structure in addition provides terrific quality protection as a results of it separates the business from the individual.

long assets square measure typically command by different liability companies which will use accounting methods higher fitted to investments. All assets square measure protected against creditors and so the legal liabilities of the individual as a results of their command by separate legal entities. the quantity of legal protection is set by state law. many advisors counsel forming these entities in states which will not alter the piercing of the legal structure. Most like Battle Born State as a results of its lack of company excise, flexibility to charge orders as a sole remedy by creditors, the obscurity of not having to list shareholders, and so the nomination of company officers.

Although mercantilism through a fancy legal structure has obvious edges, it also can add a serious amount of quality to one's personal affairs. For merchants square measure consistently profitable but cannot or do not want to qualify for merchant standing, mercantilism through a simple business is very important. If you wish to line up a pension fund to defer taxes, pay salaries to pet ones or recoup vital medical expenses tax-free, then the added quality is also an honest trade-off to appreciate the benefits of a compound structure. Either way, to receive the best tax treatment and legal protection, speak with advisors understand the formation and operation of these entities for traders.

Of course passive money gains square measure a couple of things most of the folks would adore. Wouldn't a bit like the set up of making money whereas you are out having associate honest time? nonetheless traditionally day mercantilism has been thought of an active, long suggests that of generating profits.

Being able to day trade for a living successfully suggests that reaching tier of targeted excellence that nearly all of us will never deliver the products, however what career they choose. It's the excellence between being a movie extra associate degreed associate Oscar-winning actor or between collaborating in in associate extremely pick-up outdoor game inside the park and being the Superbowl participant.

The point is not to discourage someone from following their dream, but it's necessary, if you would like to pursue day mercantilism for a living, to travel into it along side your eyes wide open.

Spend some serious time educating yourself relating to everything you will be able to be related to mercantilism. presumably, you would like to be daily businessperson rummage around for short gains, not academic degree capitalist seeking long profits, so place inside the hours necessary to gift yourself a strong understanding of the earth you are on the purpose of enter. The Securities and Exchange Commission (SEC), the financial business administrative unit (FINRA), and so the revenue Service (IRS) all offer valuable information for day traders. Introductory books on ways in which and theories will assist you get familiar with the collaborating in field.

To get started mercantilism, you will got to develop a sound mercantilism methodology, one that takes advantage of volatility, nonetheless invariably keeps risk management as its core principle. Ideally, this system got to be tested over months or years, altogether utterly completely different market environments, initial with a demo account thus with real money.

Financially, many veteran traders counsel having a minimum of 1 year's value of monetary gain forgot before you start. usually | this will be} often not the bankroll {that you | that you merely | that you just} simply can trade with— you will would love separate capital for that, in amounts that fluctuate depending on the sort of day mercantilism you will do—but money {that you | that you merely | that you just} simply will use to pay your living expenses, along side for housing, insurance, and food.

Having this financial cushion will give you with peace of mind, allowing you to begin your new career whereas not the pressure of about to trade to "make the rent." you will be in addition got to have a recordkeeping strategy ready for tax season.

Psychologically, you got to steel yourself for the gain inconsistency which will attainable accompany your mercantilism. The goal once mercantilism for a living is to possess a reliable and consistent revenue stream, but which will take time, diligence, and luck to appreciate. Having in reality the daily fluctuations of your gain square measure typically sturdy on the psyche over time.

The speed, fluctuations, adrenaline, and comparatively high quantitative relation relative to wins can produce investment a jarring experience for fresh day traders. This runs against the essential human impulse to "win" the utmost quantity as possible. you will would love patience and cool-headedness; otherwise, the strain of day mercantilism can bring disturbance on your emotional well-being.

These square measure variety of the essential things to recollect of if you are about to decide to produce a living mercantilism stocks. And though' the chances square measure against your success, if you are one in every of the few can master this art, you will get pleasure from excitement, independence, and financial rewards.

Fortunately, fashionable technology presently permits folks to some extent, to need a back seat and still manufacture a profit. However, you wish to note a system that suits your individual circumstances, whereas in addition considering the risks and any tax rules.

Now {that you|that you merely|that you just} simply have scan this book, you need to be in associate extremely higher position to make a turn whether or not or not or not day mercantilism is correct for you. Day mercantilism desires a definite perspective, furthermore as a discipline and a set of skills that no person possesses. curiously, most of the traders i do recognize are poker players. They get pleasure from speculation and so the stimulation that comes from it. tho' poker is also a sort of gambling, day mercantilism is not. Day mercantilism is also a science, a skill, and a career, and has nothing to do to with gambling. it is the intense business of mercantilism and buying stocks, usually in associate extremely matter of seconds. you need to be able to produce selections fast, with no feeling or hesitation. Doing otherwise winds up in losing real money

Once you have a simulated account, you will got to develop your strategy. try the ways in which I even have mentioned throughout this book, and master one or a pair of of them. VWAP, Support or Resistance, and Reversal ways in which square measure the best. you'd wish to exclusively master a handful of of them to invariably be profitable inside the market. Keep your strategy easy. once you have got a solid strategy that you've down, make sure there isn't any feeling connected to that.

Practice with the amounts of money {that you|that you merely|that you just} simply square measure planning to be mercantilism in world. it's easy to buy for a grip value $100,000 {in a|during a|in an extremely|in a very}n exceedingly simulated account and watch it lose 1/2 its value in a matter of seconds. but might you tolerate this loss in associate extremely real account? If not, you will possibly become academic degree emotional businessperson and make a decision quickly, generally resulting in a significant loss. Invariably trade with the scale and position {that you|that you merely|that you just} simply square measure planning to be utilised inside the $64000 account. Otherwise, {there's no|there is no|there isn't associatey|there is not any} purpose in mercantilism in an extremely simulated account. Move to a real account once a minimum of three months of work with a simulated account thus, begin very little, with real money. Trade very little whereas you're learning or once you're feeling stressed. Continue your education and replicate upon your mercantilism strategy. never stop learning relating to the stock market. It's a dynamic setting and it's constantly dynamical. Day mercantilism is totally completely different than it had been ten years ago, and it will vary in another ten years. so keep reading and discussing your progress and performance with mentors and different traders. invariably suppose ahead and maintain a progressive perspective. Learn the utmost quantity as you will be able to, but keep a degree of healthy skepticism relating to everything, along side this book. Raise queries, and do not accept consultants at their word.

Join a community of traders. mercantilism alone is very robust and should be emotionally overwhelming. it's very helpful to hitch a community of traders so you will be able to raise them queries, visit them, learn new ways and ways, get some hints and alerts relating to the stock market, and in addition produce your own contributions. If you be a district of American state, you will see that I generally lose money. it's typically comforting to see that losing money is not restricted to you, and everyone, along side veteran traders, should take a loss. As I've said, it's all a district of the tactic. There square measure many chatrooms {that you|that you merely|that you just} simply are a district of on the net. variety of them square measure free, but most of them charge a fee. By connexion our data processor (for free),

You got to not follow the pack but ought to be academic degree freelance thinker. Generally, of us modification once they be a district of crowds. They become loads of unquestioning and impulsive, nervously searching for a frontrunner whose trades they're going to mirror. They react with the gang instead of applying their minds. data processor members would possibly catch a handful of trends on, but they get killed once trends reverse. perpetually bear in mind that booming traders square measure freelance thinkers. simply use your judgment to create a choice once to trade and once to not.

Pick a market you are fascinated by and would possibly afford to trade. Then, set yourself up with the right instrumentality and package. choose a time of day {that you|that you merely|that you just} simply will day trade and exclusively trade throughout that time; usually the foremost effective day commerce times square measure around major market openings and closings. Manage your risk, on every trade and each day. Then, apply a way over and another time.

You ought to not perceive everything to trade profit. you would like to be able to implement one strategy that makes money.

Focus on winning with one strategy before attempting to seek out out others. Hone your skills in associate extremely demo account; but perceive that it is not specifically like real commerce. Once you turn to mercantilism with real capital, a jarring ride is common for several months. think about truth and implementation to steady your nerves.

www.ingramcontent.com/pod-product-compliance
Lightning Source LLC
Chambersburg PA
CBHW070650220526
45466CB00001B/378